JOY is My Job

ISBN: 979-8-218-27528-0

Printed in the United States of America

If you are passing a bit of joy on to a friend,
below is a spot for you to write a joy-filled wish for them.

Dear Friend,

Joyfully Yours

Dear Friend,

Imagine you are sitting in a room full of people, at a round table with crispy white linens. In front of you is a fancy dinner setting and a champagne flute filled with bubbly. Someone at the front of the room holds a microphone in one hand and a glass in the other. They say to the room full of people, "If you are living a life full of joy, the kind where you regularly smile and laugh and feel alive...where life feels more light than it does heavy, please stand up."

Now I must know...Would you be able to authentically and proudly stand?

Welcome to the introduction letter of Joy is My Job! I am so excited that you have picked up a copy and I hope you find it as joyful and entertaining as I envisioned when I sat down to write.

I wrote this book as the next step for anyone (especially women) looking to add more joy to their lives. If YOU are any of these things, this book is for you:

1. I consider my life joyfilled and still, I want more! *Yes, you deserve it!*
2. I have a lot of crap in my life that gets in the way, but I still want joy. *All the crap is real, like real-real, and you are exactly right, you should find joy, in between all of the chaos of life!*
3. I am feeling a little bit discouraged and could use a bit of jet fuel for my life. *Don't worry, I've got ideas and inspiration for you! joy is going to be your new best-friend!*

I am deeply passionate about helping people realize and wholeheartedly believe that joy is their job and I'm consumed with the idea that you are capable of more joy than you have ever imagined. I know for a fact because I have been chasing joy like it's my job for seven years, and have countless stories, strategies, and memories as proof. If you are ready to push yourself past the day-to-day humdrum and knock down the "life stuff" that gets in the way of creating joy, then let's go!! I know you will find and create joy to last a lifetime.

joyfully yours,

Lisa Even

Joy Connoisseur

A Quick Joy Check-in

Joy Check In

I have left you a copy of the joy Check-in Worksheet at the beginning and end of this book. Take a moment to see who and where you are now regarding joy, and then compare that to the person you are after reading Joy is My Job. You can continue to use this worksheet going forward as a way to determine whether you need to prioritize joy.

Creating more joy tomorrow starts with where you are at today. Take time to reflect on the current status of your joy, and then answer the three questions below. The answers to these questions will be the catalyst for building a life filled with joy!

(1) What are currently the top three things that get in your way of having joy?

1. _____

2. _____

3. _____

(2) If you were to look ahead one year from now, what area(s) of your life would you want to see more joy in?

_____

_____

_____

_____

_____

_____

On a scale of 1-10, where are you <u>currently</u> with joy for the categories that apply to you?

	LOW (little JOY) ☹					HIGH (lots of JOY!) ☺				
YOURSELF	1	2	3	4	5	6	7	8	9	10
IN MARRIAGE (Or Relationship)	1	2	3	4	5	6	7	8	9	10
W/ KIDS	1	2	3	4	5	6	7	8	9	10

If your score is lower than you want it to be, this is a sign that joy has fallen to the bottom of the heap. Think about what, where, and how you might add more joyful activities to your life.

Where you would be a year from now is a reflection of the choices you make right now.

JOY is My Job

LISA EVEN

A book to spark joy filled mindset, moments, and experiences!

Dedication

To my kids.
May you always make joy your Job.

Special Thanks

To my husband, Loras.

You are the joy in my life and I couldn't imagine a better advocate and life adventure partner.

To Alaina (9 years old) and Sawyer (11 years old), and Ana Dellamuth (kid at heart) for the artwork and handwriting in this book.

To Kyle Calvert for a fantastically joyful cover design.

YOUR FREE GIFT

Thank you so much for deciding to add more JOY to your life. To thank you for being amazing, I wanted to give you this gift.

You can find it here: https://www.lisaeven.com/freejoy

Contents

Introduction

I found joy when...

I'd like to say that the concept of making joy My Job started while I sat leisurely sipping a steamy hot cup of coffee on the patio of a trendy coffee shop without a care in the world, but in reality, it was birthed by desperation seven years ago. It was the middle of the week and my husband and I were sitting in our living room, him in a chair and me on the couch, watching TV around 7:45 pm, just a few minutes after we had gotten our kids into bed. The kitchen sink was full of dishes and there was a basket or two of laundry waiting for my attention, but my usually scheduled self was done for the day. I had quickly thrown on comfy clothes and was now perched directly in the center of the couch, a glass of wine in my hand and a bowl of popcorn in front of me. I remember feeling exhausted from a packed day of meetings (I'm sure he was too). It had been a long week for both of us with work and kids...all the things. The plan was to watch a bit of TV, zone out and try to unravel our stress, and then call it a day. I made sure to dump all of the remaining "to-do" items on a scratch piece of paper on the counter using my son's green marker before making my way over to the living room. This would be the placeholder and proof that I had not failed to complete the housework, but rather I was just re-scheduling it for the morning. Ha, see...I'm in total control, I thought.

After a few minutes of mindlessly watching Netflix and feeling a little angry with myself about my severe level of tiredness, I looked at my husband, who was looking at the TV like a zombie, and said, "When will we feel like we've 'made it'?" He looked at me for a minute with a confused and thoughtful sort-of expression and said, "I am not sure..." I could tell from his face that we were thinking the same thing.

More Netflix flashed across the screen (I wish I could remember what trashy and somewhat pointless show we were watching) and then I sat up quickly, almost spilling my wine and popcorn, and said, "We've been doing (or have done) everything we were 'supposed to'...we went to college and got our degrees, bought a house (which did feel like a series of endless projects), sold the house, have been climbing the ladder at work, and had the kids. But instead of feeling this huge sense of relief and accomplishment like we thought we would when we got to the finish line of each of those things, we feel like we have less uumph in us, are no closer to our goals (whatever the hell that means), and we are over-scheduled and uninspired." I felt like I had just given a rousing commencement speech, and maybe a tiny piece of me knew I was. In a way, I was petitioning for a change, and he laughed. He looked at me with an expression that said...*yes, you are right* but he didn't say anything.

"Hear me out," I said. "We schedule everything: work meetings, personal appointments, meetings, kids activities, when our extended family is going to visit, when to change the furnace filter, and even when to give the dog (an adorably pudgy black and brown dachshund) her heartworm medicine. And we have no problem chasing our tail to make all of these things happen! What if we could chase joy, chase it like it's our job instead of chasing our jobs like they are our jobs?"

His eyebrows went up this time and he started laughing. I was hesitant to keep going, for fear he thought I had jumped off the deep end, but I did. "What if we could flip the whole nonsense of it all and we make the CHOICE of what we give our brain space to? Be laser-focused on the pieces of our life that we want to make better. What if we actually create a list of fun things to do and then SCHEDULE our joy? I am just afraid that if we keep running on the hamster wheel that we are on, joy may never find US; my gut says we have to find IT."

Now that I had his attention and maybe his curiosity, he said, "How do we do it?" I thought for a minute and then responded, "Well, first we need a list of ideas. Then we could look at our month and ask ourselves the question, where can we put more joy? I think we should put joy inside and around everything in our lives...make it our job to find joy! Basically, we try to design our lives so that we have more of what we love...what do you think!?" He laughed again and this time I could see he had become more interested in the thought of it. "Yeah, we should do that. Sounds like it wouldn't take too much effort to get that going."

The following week I bought a large whiteboard from Home Depot and lugged it up the stairs of our apartment building and asked my husband to hang it on our bedroom wall. He gave me a weird look as though he thought I was crazy (honestly, I might have been a little bit crazy, but I was determined). Later that day I convinced him to tackle our new project and he teased me as we hung the whiteboard on the wall adjacent to our bed, saying people don't hang whiteboards in their bedrooms....but because he is a great guy, he hung it anyway. I told him this was the ideal location for two reasons: 1) so our kids can't get to it and erase everything and 2) because sometimes the only time we have together is before bed and I want us to brainstorm our joy ideas before we fall asleep. Hopefully we will dream about joy too! In laughing agreement, we stood back at our new bedroom "art" and I said, "Let operation joy is our j-o-b begin!"

Now, much of this book was written at Starbucks, the only quiet place a working-from-home parent truly has...am I right? And some of it was written in airports while traveling for work. On one particular trip, I took one of the last remaining seats at my gate at the Dallas, TX airport, squishing in between a family on my left (kids sitting quietly watching their devices) and a woman traveling alone to my right. My seat was facing the middle of the terminal and since we were delayed for nearly 45 minutes, I waited patiently and watched as people got up from their seats to use the restroom, buy coffee and snacks, or walk laps with their young toddlers; so many laps! One toddler-parent pair caught my eye, a tall slim dad with a baseball cap and his adorable and very chatty daughter, who looked close to four years old. He had a black backpack on and her miniature hello kitty backpack slung over his shoulder, a pink booster seat in his left hand, and in his right, he was pulling a small bright pink hard case suitcase with a unicorn painted on the side. His daughter sat on top, looking like she was riding the unicorn. I smiled. After each lap, I could hear him ask her, "Are you done? Or should we go around again?" And the answer was always a loud and bright, "YES! Another lap!"

On one of their final loops, I could hear her saying in a happy and excited voice, "Daddy, pull me along so I can keep up!" For some reason, this moment reminded me of the joy that our family has been chasing and curating over the past seven years and I smiled because sometimes the days have truly felt like that...just a series of laps. And from time to time, one of us pauses to remind the other that we need to keep going. YES! Another lap! It also reminds me that there are even more times when one of us has to do a little tugging and pulling and dragging the other along a bit, much like that exuberant toddler saying, "Pull me along so I can keep up!"

Like many, I feel the invisible burdens. The never-ending task list at work and home. The feeling that you are the "default" parent, the one remembering everything: appointments, uniforms, water bottles, lunches, picture day, sports, and school sign-ups all while endlessly feeling that you are never going to catch up, or worse, feeling like it's a lost battle altogether. But what I have learned is that the minute we give all of our energy to our task lists thinking that we will "get ahead" someday (when the reality is that we will NEVER fully catch up), things seem more burdensome and it is difficult to see the forest through the trees. Hell, the trees feel like they are closing in and around us and are somehow holding us hostage.

It takes grit to live in a world that is a moving target and to be able to:

- Not let your task list define you
- Keep up with housework and work to an appropriate level
- Know that you will always have something left to do
- Realizing that you are doing the best you can and that is perfect
- That progress is sometimes so small that it is hard to notice

I do occasionally slip up and let my task list overtake me because, well, I am human. My mind sinks to the point where I can't see past the piles of work (and the fingerprints on the fridge and toothpaste streaks on the mirror) and I start or end sentences with a quip about how much work I have done or have left to do, continuously running my to-do list over in my head. I start telling my brain to conserve energy, knowing that I am going to need "all I can get" to make it through the day. If that is you too, I get it. It's much easier to take the approach that you have nothing else to give.

Sadly, this is where most parents (especially women) stay for a good period of their young family years and sometimes it starts even before they have kids. In this "just get by mode," they look forward to better days ahead...once my kids are sleeping through the night, or when they are in school, or when they are (insert the next milestone). And before they know it, they have been in that mode for so long that they cannot remember what it felt like to feel alive and joyful.

And the stats confirm it. A recent Forbes article statistic found that 53 percent of women say their stress levels are higher than a year ago, and almost half feel burned out. One-third have taken time off work because of mental health (nodding head). Another article from the Harvard Business Review talks about the dangers of micro stresses, the small moments of stress that seem manageable on their own – "think a vague, worrying text from your teen flashing on your phone while you are in a meeting, the appearance of a colleague who always wants to vent to you, or having to tell your team that the project you have all been grinding out extra hours on is no longer a priority. But these micro-stresses are not as harmless as they seem. Because they are so small and brief, they don't trigger the normal stress response in our brains to help us cope; instead, micro-stress embeds itself in our minds and accrues over time. The long-term impact of this buildup is debilitating: It saps our energy, damages our physical and emotional health, and contributes to a decline in our overall well-being."

Whatever your current situation, I promise you that you are not alone. We, the parents around the world, get it. These micro-stresses are causing chaos and exhaustion. We have lived it and the mental burden is real. We, too, feel like we are in the middle of an ocean on a small yellow blow-up raft with a lifejacket that is strangling us just slightly with turbulent waves, the water washing over us and knocking us over in our seats. Just as the waves let up, the sun comes out and after the sun sufficiently burns us, then droopy rain clouds appear to douse us with rain...it's a never-ending cycle of tackling the next challenge.

Whatever your next milestone or mission, I want you to know that you do not need to suffer through it, and certainly not alone. There are ways to infuse joy into the most challenging of times and it does not have to be hard, time-consuming, or feel like it is another thing on the list. There is so much untapped potential for creating more micro joy in your world and it starts with a desire for more. A desire to laugh more, to enjoy the company of your family and friends more, to feel alive more. I believe each one of us has an opportunity to redesign our lives with joy at the forefront.

We have been conditioned to think that we have to do it ALL and be everything to everyone...make a better meal for our family, when what they crave is just us...the version that does not think too much about whether it will be good enough or what else is on the list. They don't care if their house is tidy or if the bathroom is clean and they won't remember whether it was on any given day. It's easy to say, "Well if I don't do it, who will," and I ask you to put that aside for a moment and ask yourself, "What does a life without joy gain me?"

This book is filled with tactical advice, ideas, and strategies. I wanted it to be actionable and easy. I am not an expert in the psychology of joy, but I am someone who realized that life is too short to leave joy on the table. I have tried many ways to create more joy and what it came down to is this:

1. Mindset – the things I tell myself, the justification I use in the moment.
2. Barriers to joy – the real-life stuff that gets in the way and how to persevere.
3. Joy in action – the quick list of ideas, challenges, and an actual calendar that help me keep joy on the forefront.

I have written about my experience with creating more joy and I am excited to share it with you! I want you to get excited about the joy you create, knock down the barriers that get in your way of having joy, and leave with quick and easy marching orders on how to infuse more joy into your day-to-day life.

I have included a guilt-free framework for creating joy that anyone can use and I have tested the concept with high school students, working professionals of many ages in 20+ industries, retirees, and of course, my family. I am confident that if you follow a few key steps, you will see significant gains in the joy ROI (return on investment) you get. Are you ready to live a more joyful life? HELL YES, Let's Go!

Joy Comes from the Hard Stuff

My grandma made the best ice cream shakes, and she would make us one every time we visited (which was often). When I was about 13 or 14 years old, while eating a chocolate shake out of a glass at her kitchen counter, I remember her telling me that once my grandfather retired from farming, they were going to travel and go on many adventures. When I hit high school, unfortunately, my grandparents got sick one right after the other. My grandfather had colon cancer which did not heal well and then after he recovered, the brain tumor he had since childhood started to grow and cause problems. He had always been active and healthy (minus the significant hearing loss that caused us to yell in his direction) but slowly started becoming frail.

My grandmother who had been at his side the entire time started complaining about her eyesight, blaming her prescription glasses. New pairs of glasses did not seem to fix the problem and slowly her balance started to go; she would hold onto furniture and sway slightly when standing unassisted. Doctors could not seem to pinpoint what was causing her symptoms and finally, she was diagnosed with a neurological disease called PSP, which causes the brainstem to slowly deteriorate, a terrible disease.

I would drop cards in the mail and when I was back from college and visited on weekends, I would notice the slow decline occurring. My mom and her siblings had now become the full-time caregivers for both my grandparents, and over the years, the caregiving burdens grew and grew. A year after college, I was engaged to be married and I asked my grandfather to walk me half way down the aisle. It was going to be a challenge for him, as walking had become a struggle, but he gladly agreed and said it gave him something to look forward to. Unfortunately, my grandma passed away a few months before my wedding and my grandfather, a few weeks before the big day. He had gone to Hallmark a few months before with my aunt and I remember crying big alligator tears during the gift opening, the day after my wedding, when I unwrapped the china dishes he had bought. I never wish sadness on anyone, but I remember saying in passing to my new husband, that we need to do fun things while we can.

My grandparents' illnesses were around the time of the unexpected deaths of my cousins. Dean, a jovial and kind soul, who was more hardworking and loyal than anyone I know...He did two tours in the Army (Afghanistan and Iraq) and was beyond proud to keep our country safe. Erin, a hilarious and adventurous fun 22-year-old. I can still see her bright smile and hear her laugh echoing through the house, remember watching her play basketball and thinking she was as good as Michael Jordan (I'm going to be just like her when I grow up, I thought), and trips to get ice cream at our local Dairy Queen in her giant old green car. Their deaths most certainly helped shape the way I see the world today. Lisa, there is no time to waste...life is short!

A BIG part of me is inspired to create joy because my grandparents and cousins cannot anymore. These were some of the worst moments I can remember and yet, they are also some of the most influential. I am sure somewhere in your background, there is a story, memory, or a person who did not get their chance to fully live. I hope you use their story(s), as positive jet fuel for your joy journey, an in-the-moment perspective shift. When the weight of the day feels heavy and you are debating whether you can squeeze in some joy, these stories are what will become your north star...head in that direction and create joy because they cannot.

These world-shattering experiences created a not-so-silent undercurrent for the next 20 years of my life (almost a tidal wave). When I feel like I have nothing more to give, they remind me that I am still here...and that means there is still joy to be had.

We will spend time in this book talking about what gets in the way of joy (time, your task list, money, housework, the burden of planning, etc.) and how to shift our mindset to the idea that we can get things done

AND have joy. I will also provide quick and easy joy ideas that you can go out and do. I hope you leave feeling energized and realize that:

- o Life is short
- o You happen to the world, not the other way around!
- o Joy is your job

PART 1

Mindset

Joy is a Choice

The first time I noticed a difference in people's happiness or joy levels was when I worked at our local cafe in high school called R&R. The cafe was long and narrow, probably 15 feet across and 40 feet long. The walls were sponge-painted and lace curtains hung in the front windows. We had one of those plastic open and closed signs that hung on the glass door, and each weekend morning I would flip it to show that we were ready for business. A line of customers would stream in shortly after, proudly saying they had already been to the gas station for a first cup and were ready for a second. My teenage self thought they were crazy! Why would anyone get up that early?! This was when you could smoke indoors and so a light haze quickly covered the ceiling. To one side was a long counter with light brown leather-topped bar stools, a narrow aisle, and then a long row of tables with thick plastic table cloths, jelly caddies, and glass salt and pepper shakers. In total, there were six or seven barstools and eight tables that held around 30-40 people max.

I started working there when I was 14 years old, washing dishes in the tiny kitchen. Nothing will teach you about hard work better than the service industry, am I right?! At 15, I was promoted from dishwasher to waitress, which was much more lucrative in many ways (money and the number of lessons that came with it). Locals would pony up to the counter for cup after cup of coffee, farmers and truckers would grab an early morning breakfast before heading out to the fields, retirees would come in to read the paper, and mid-morning we would get a rush of families with kids.

I was curious about all of the different people that came in...What were their lives like? What did they do after they left the café? Some customers were 30, 40, 50+ years older than me. It's funny how I am now one of those "old people," and I laugh because back then I couldn't imagine what it would be like to be "old." I learned a LOT about the lives of the "regulars," all about their careers, what was keeping them busy in retirement, the number of kids and grandkids they had, what it was like "back in their day," hobbies and interests, and of course their temperaments and preferences (stop by often and keep their coffee hot).

I got to know who I could joke around with and who I couldn't. Sometimes customers would sit there for hours chatting about the weather and the news and all the "happenings" in our small town. Many of them came in each weekend and I could rattle off the specifics of their orders...dry toast, decaf coffee with cream, extra gravy on their biscuits, and two glasses of water with ice. I also got to know their temperaments and general view on life. Some seemed truly energized no matter their circumstance:

- Lloyd, a partially blind retiree, would come into the coffee shop wearing sunglasses complaining that it was "too bright" in here.

- Bob, a semi-truck driver who would be gone for long stretches at a time, would come back with stories and be curious about what I was up to in school and sports. Always reminding me to be careful out there!

- Ray, an energetic auto body shop owner originally from England, was always cracking jokes, playing tricks, and pretending to complain about the service.

- Joe, owner of a local tow truck company, would come in with a toothpick hanging out the side of his mouth. He became a phone-a-friend whenever any one of the waitresses' cars needed a tow out of a ditch...it's up to you whether you tell your parents, he would say with a wink.

- My Grandpa Bill and all of his "coffee buddies" would play a game with a dollar bill, where whoever could guess the first two numbers of the dollar's serial number was the lucky winner who had to buy coffee for the entire group! You could hear their cheers from outside the café when the winner was announced. I have never seen anyone so happy to NOT win a game!

- Others, who just wanted to reminisce and share stories about their past or even present (lots and lots of life advice and grandkid stories).

Some people who came into the café seemed less energized and visibly cranky. I remember one older gentleman in a John Deere hat who asked me what my plans were after high school, telling me that I will go to the big city and come right back because nobody ever makes it out of this town. Others who, when you made a mistake on their order, would send the food back and say to their friends in a less than helpful tone, "You can't get good service around here anymore." I noticed these types of people were negative about most things...their food, the conversations they were having, the final report of...."Well, I better get going and deal with (insert negative description of their upcoming day)."

It dawned on me that joy might be something we choose, similar to the outfit we wear each day. I started to entertain the idea that a person puts on their attitude, just like they put on their clothes. This idea stuck with me because even now with our friend group, we will remind people to bring their "party pants" when we get together.

I'm not sure I gave much notice to the type of person I wanted to BE or NOT BE at the time, but as I got to college, things became a little clearer. I realized that those joyful and cranky people were EVERYWHERE, not just in the small corner of Iowa where I had served coffee and breakfast.

I remember a few of my college professors who would get so excited about their content that they would get white board marker streaks on their face or their hair would be tussled by the end of class, or they would not even realize that class was over...almost making us leave late. And even though I sometimes didn't enjoy the content, I was more interested and probably learned a hell of a lot more because they were excited about the material —in so many words, they were joyful about their jobs. I just ate up the fact that they were so eager about their topic, which got me excited about the topic (it was contagious). Other professors droned on, made unpleasant remarks about the world, and would be less than friendly to students. My hypothesis was confirmed once again, joy is something we wear and it's a choice.

Guess what? After college, those same joyful and unjoyful people were there too! My first job out of college was at a staffing company where I processed paperwork for physicians to be able to work in emergency rooms. Our industry, recruitment and staffing for healthcare, was hard by nature because it was a constant churn of finding more people to work more shifts at more places. Not for the faint of heart. The job wore on a lot of our team members and created some bitter people. But at the same time, it didn't. Some people were joyful even through the yuck and the muck. There would be days when we had to stay late or had a tight deadline. Sometimes the person we thought might pick up a shift to work would not, and I remember one of the senior leaders at that organization did not waiver, they were calm and quietly positive. When I asked him how he kept so positive and dealt with the stress, he responded, "Joy is a choice, one that I make each day, through the good and the bad." I walked out of his office a bit intrigued.

Making the Case for Joy

A young woman named Kelsey gave a commencement speech at her graduation from NC State that included one of the most profound things I have ever heard. She began by telling a story about how a traumatic brain injury from softball, during her time as a student, ended her athletic career and almost her academic career as well. The injury left her struggling with daily tasks, stuttering, and confusion, and she could no longer prove herself through performance of any kind. The external labels that she had built her entire identity around (athlete and student) were broken.

She urged her classmates to think about their lives not in the "doing" but rather in the "being." "Yes, the jobs we will accept after graduation are important (engineer, teacher, doctor), but as I have learned through having my softball career taken away that it's more about the 'being.'" Learn to describe yourself and others by their attitude, how they treat others, and what makes them uniquely beautiful...it's the individual characteristics and not the things they do, but who they ARE.

Sometimes it's easy to think to ourselves that joy can wait because of the doing: we have so much to accomplish and are flooded with the busy, tired, work, kids, and money. But it's instances like Kelsey's that remind us that our doing is not the actual measure of success in life, but rather our being. I encourage you to consider these four reasons why joy should happen in the "being" of life.

1) We all need reinforcements when life is tough

When my kids were very little, I remember I would think that going to work was a break. I could have a few moments where someone wasn't needing something right NOW. Where I could wear a shirt longer than four hours because nothing had been wiped or spilled on it (minus the oatmeal splotch on my shoulder from my son who hugged me each morning at daycare and would always leave a bit of breakfast on my shoulder as he laid his head down). Some days I miss that splotch. Those days were long and my husband, who was still in school, was around very little.

Joy props us up through all life's moments and provides the hope we need to keep going.

What got us through those zombie days (as we like to call them) were the things we had coming up: living room date nights after the kids were in bed, new parks to try out, and shows to watch. When there was no time to go and create joy, we would imagine ourselves back on the beach from a vacation we had taken years back. Or a funny story about the time we stayed out all night and now, we were getting up at the time we used to go to bed.

Life can be tough (so unbearably hard that sometimes we aren't sure if we are going to make it through), and without having something to look back on (memories and moments) or look forward to (things coming up, the bright spots on our calendar), things feel heavy. And if things feel heavy, we are less hopeful, less motivated, less creative, and less productive. All the tasks we need to complete occur more slowly. Two of my favorite sayings are, "Everything is temporary" and "Someday we'll look back and laugh," meaning the moment today will pass.

The best visual I can give to anyone is to imagine yourself standing in-between two buildings. The buildings are so close together that you can <u>almost</u> touch both with your arms outstretched, but your arms don't touch either by just an inch or so. The building to the left is the joy in your past—all the things you have experienced. The building to the right is the joy you are planning for in the future. Standing directly in the middle is you. There will come a time when standing will feel hard and you will have to lean to the left or right. If today is not a good day, you must lean on one of the buildings—the past or your future—to remind yourself that joy is possible. It's coming...you know this because you have had it before. Joy props us up through all life's moments and provides the hope we need to keep going.

2) There are no do-overs

Have you ever considered that your job is not to create a good future for your family (or self), but rather give them a good "past"? To create moments (today, tomorrow, and the next day) that are joyful and worth remembering. You cannot get the past back and if you fill your days with hustle and bustle without any joy, you are missing out.

I feel this great sense of urgency to create joy, spread joy, and inspire joy because of (as I already mentioned) the people I have lost. Those moments taught me that life is fragile and that there are no do-overs, no promises of tomorrows, but only todays.

I once heard a story where a mom asks her adult daughter, who is getting ready to have surgery, what meal she should bring over to the house after she is home recovering. The daughter without skipping a beat says, tuna casserole. The mom, looking appalled, says, "Why in the world would you want that? Out of all the things that you could pick!"

The daughter responds, "It reminds me of childhood, it's a comfort food. You always used to make it for us." The mom turns and says, "I always made it for you at the end of the month because it was cheap, it's what I could afford."

Isn't it funny that the things you do daily that seem insignificant can bring someone joy? Be on the lookout for the little moments and the things that your family and friends enjoy (conversation topics, games you play together, things that you cook, the car dance parties, hide and seek in the basement), these are the mini-moments that they carry forward with them on the journey of life.

Your job isn't to make the best or most expensive experience for your family but rather to give them a moment to remember, a moment to savor. I love hearing my kids say, "Remember last month when...remember last week when..." because I know that I am taking advantage of today. As the quote goes, "Yesterday's history, tomorrow's a mystery, today's a gift...that's why we call it the present."

3) Joy is contagious

My morning commute used to be 45 minutes long. I would travel from a northern suburb of Milwaukee, WI to a southern suburb, via a very busy (and usually under construction) highway. Though four lanes were going in each direction, there was often stop-and-go traffic along the route. I remember one morning, I spent an additional 30 minutes crawling along next to orange construction pylons and by the time I walked into the hospital where I worked, I felt exhausted from having to focus and hold my hands steady for so long.

I stopped at the Starbucks just inside the hospital door and was again greeted by another line of what felt like stop-and-go coffee traffic. I finally got to the register and was greeted by the barista. I think he could tell that I was having "a morning" and asked me if he could tell me a coffee joke. I agreed, thinking as long as you make it fast, and as he poured more water into the coffee machine, he said: RIP, boiling water. You will be mist. I could not help but laugh out loud and feel my commuting frustration go down.

Joy is contagious. When you create it for the people around you, they will be compelled to create joy too. I think I told six or seven people the joke that day and made sure to tell my husband that evening, and years later, now I am telling you. It's amazing how far something so tiny, but so good (or bad) can travel.

It's a mission of mine to be joyfully contagious. Recently, I got a card in the mail that said:

Lisa

After hearing you speak at our corporate holiday party, I brought my joy calendar home to my husband. We have been married for almost 19 years, and 4 kids later, quality time became playing on our phones in the same room 10 feet apart. We started our joy dates on December 31st and have completed 8. When I tell you that this has re-sparked the joy in my marriage, I'm not kidding. We talk so much more. We feel like we are dating again. This has now led us both to create our own "My Personal Joy" calendars to find our joy for ourselves. Thank you for your inspiration.

My goal for you is to be contagious to the people you love (even the ones you don't) and the people you meet. Be the joyful version (your version, not mine) that you were meant to be. Every person, whether soft-spoken or loud, introverted or extroverted, wants to carry a bit of joy with them...bring joy forward in your own way. There are so many people out there who bring the world down, and I know that being contagious in a good way is the only way to bring it back up.

4) I'm a better human when...

In graduate school, right around the time of my wedding, I started feeling my heart race for a few minutes at a time. It would happen without warning and I could not figure out why. One night after dinner, I frantically told my husband we should go to the hospital because I was afraid I was having a heart attack. It was one of the scariest car rides I have taken (besides when I was in labor with my two kids) and when we arrived at the hospital, the staff hooked me up to all sorts of machines for testing.

We were there for over an hour and the doctor walked into my stall (the little room that had a curtain for a door), sat down on a rolling stool, and said, "Tell me about things in your life." I looked at him skeptically and began to list everything I was doing: wedding planning, graduate school, a full-time job, ailing grandparents (stressed parents), and a wiener dog who recently had back surgery. He nodded and wrote something on his clipboard, which made me slightly nervous. He then asked about how I had been doing with sleeping, eating, exercising, plus a number of other things. I answered each question and then he turned and said, "The good news is that you are not having a heart attack," but rather premature ventricular contractions. PVCs are extra heart beats that feel like fluttering, which can be caused by stress. I looked at him in disbelief. Was I really that stressed? I had not thought I was stressed, but now that he mentioned it...I did have a lot going on. Hmmm...

The doctor's prescribed cure was rest and to go and do something fun. He told me I sounded like I had a lot on my plate and that I should make time for rest and fun (less work, more play). He smiled, shook my hand and said, "Lisa, I think you are going to be more than alright with making a few small changes." I wish I could say I was a compliant patient, but I was not. I went back to the day-to-day and very little changed. I kept being busy and stressed, and then we added kids into the mix. Though I did not end up back at the hospital, and I did a better job of not getting too stressed to where my heart would flutter, it took a few years (approximately 7 or 8) before I understood what he truly meant. It was the night on the couch, with popcorn and wine, where I told my husband we should stop chasing and start living, that I understood the prescribed treatment meant, chase joy like your job, NOT your job like it's your job.

Curating Joy

Fast forward to parenthood and it has been fun to see the evolution of joy as the kids have gone from tiny humans to elementary age. Their ability to brainstorm joy ideas and cure their boredom ('cause we know there are a lot of *I'm bored* moments) has been entertaining. Whenever the two of them mention they are bored, they know they will be met with our coined response.... "You're bored? Well, that means that your brain is hard at work. I bet you will get a great idea soon." And even though they roll their eyes and act a little miserable, they dream up a new game or activity after a few minutes and are VERY proud to report back on their activity of choice.

In addition to being able to curate their own joy when they are bored (most of the time), we are now seeing gains in their ability to shift their thinking during challenging or tough moments. Last Thanksgiving my husband had a few days off from work and we made our way down to St. Louis, nearly six hours away from home. Our thought was that it would be a bit warmer than Iowa, which ended up not being the case, go figure, and since there are many kid-friendly places to visit (the zoo, City Museum, the Arch, Union Station, etc.), we could spend a few days sightseeing and exploring a new city. We planned the trip using a shared note in our phones so the kids could contribute, and our itinerary shaped up to be a good mix of indoor and outdoor activities.

We arrived the day before Thanksgiving at our Airbnb, which was a really beautiful brick warehouse (10 stories tall) right across from the City Museum. Our apartment had very high ceilings with steel rafters, a big open main living area with concrete floors, space to play bean bags, and plenty of space for the kids to spread out.

There were two elevators in the building and we quickly learned that the normal passenger elevator was out of service, and we would need to use the freight elevator that had an oversized wooden gate and rusty metal door that opened from the top to bottom instead of opening left to right. We got into the freight elevator, closed the metal door and wooden gate, hit the button, and then waited....nothing happened. We waited a few more minutes and then opened the door, checked the hallway to see if anyone was around, and sure enough a fellow resident confirmed that the elevator was broken too. Since we each had a suitcase, a couple of grocery bags full of snacks, a cooler full of Thanksgiving chili and sides, and another cooler full of drinks, the trek to the 9th floor seemed impossible. We devised a plan to have the kids, with their suitcases, and my husband, with one of the coolers, take the first load up the stairs.

By the time all of our belongings were up the nine flights of stairs, we were out of breath (think hunched over with our hands on our knees), but felt proud of ourselves for making it. Kudos to my husband on most of the heavy lifting! On Thanksgiving, we went to the zoo, and in between the pouring rain, we got to see a number of different animals. By mid-afternoon, we were ready to warm up. The chili and cornbread muffins, and our Airbnb kept calling our name. It was one of the most relaxing holidays we have had, no rushing to relatives or cleaning in preparation for guests, just us. We watched a movie and everyone tucked in bed thinking that in just a few short hours we would be at the City Museum, a giant indoor playground, climbing through tunnels and caves!

However, the next morning I woke up to my husband whispering in my ear, we have to wake up! There is water coming into the apartment from the front door, it's flooding. In my groggy state, I thought I had misheard him because we were on the ninth floor of a big old warehouse, how can the apartment flood? But I had heard him correctly....There was water seeping in from the hallway at a very fast rate, the main living space had two inches of water, the bathroom was soaked, and now water was seeping into the bedroom.

We woke the kids, who were not ready to wake up yet, but they were troopers and immediately started picking their personal items up and moving all of our stuff to higher ground (on top of the bed, kitchen counter, and dining table). My mind went into "go mode" and I instructed the kids to get ready to take our stuff to the van. They changed, brushed their teeth, and got everything packed up in record time, incredible timing compared to what they normally do on a school day, ha! As we were scrambling to get everything packed, my husband and I tried to imagine where the water was coming from. The hallway was full of water too and it looked like it might be coming from a pipe at the end of the long corridor (hopefully clean water, we thought).

After we had everything ready to go down, we made the reverse trip down the 9 flights of stairs again (still no elevator) and loaded our suitcases into the van. The kids did a great job tromping through the water barefoot, we had decided to keep their one pair of shoes dry. My husband, who had an online meeting scheduled that day, decided to sit on our bed and take the meeting right in the middle of our slightly flooded apartment, while the kids and I drove to Starbucks to grab a coffee. Near Starbucks was Union Station, a neat old hotel that would be the perfect place to camp out while we waited.

I remember feeling a little surreal sitting in the giant hotel lobby, watching people check into their perfectly dry place of lodging. I was still a bit in shock that we had just had a flood on the ninth floor of our building and had moved out of our Airbnb after one night, but was very happy to be caffeinated and dry. I tried not to think about what we were going to do next, but rather enjoy the hot cup of coffee in front of me.

I knew my kids were still in shock too and I figured we should talk about what had just happened. I was somewhat surprised to hear them saying to each other, "Well, at least it wasn't as bad as _____ and I guess we will have to make lemonade, right Mom?" Good, I thought, at least they were putting it into context that things could have been worse. It seemed they knew things were going to be ok, and we could still salvage the trip. Though they were not talking specifically about joy, I was proud of them for the connections they were making. We must be in charge of our attitudes. For the next 90 minutes, they played on their phones, looked through pictures they had taken at the zoo, ate their Starbucks breakfast, and talked to the doorman at the hotel who told us some facts about the hotel's history. If anything, they certainly walked away with a story they will never forget!

I would like to think that our daily focus on joy being our job, leading up to the flood, helped us stay optimistic and strong during a tough moment. Not quite enough time has passed yet that we can look back and laugh, but it was reassuring to know that my kids will know what it feels like to be resilient and know they can contribute to any situation and make it more joyful, even the hard ones. I know there will be many tough moments in their lives and I can only hope that they pause for just a moment, think about the situation, and know it's temporary and that it's their job to make it better. Joy is their job (and yours too)!

It's been fun to start teaching our kids that joy is their job, no one else's. We know we are the example and permission-givers to our children, which is why my husband and I often talk about the choices we make as adults related to joy and impact (everything you say and do has a ripple effect, happy or crappy, it's your choice). We try to share some of the fun and easy decisions we make daily, but also a few of the tough decisions too because we want them to know that they have the power to choose how they show up and how they approach each situation and a responsibility to themselves and others to make the world a better and brighter place.

Creating a Joy Mindset

It is impossible to curate joy 24/7, but it is possible to believe that joy can happen at any time.

Permission

There are many moments when I felt like giving up and forgetting the idea of joy altogether because being joyful feels like another task (insert visual of me intensely ripping that task list up and throwing it away), and planning other things feels like work, and even remembering to make time for joy can feel like extra. And then I remember an Instagram video from *itslennnie*, where the little blob says, "Stop stompin on your seeds." If you have not seen the video, you should. Lennie says, "you don't plant a garden and tend it 24/7, every day all day, instead, you water it from time to time, here and there, and let it be and then it will do its thaaanng. Let.it.grow." I completely agree, Lennie! Joy is just like that, you need to tend it from time-to-time and let it do its thaanng.

Shifting your mindset to believe that joy is a choice, being on the lookout for moments that could use a sprig of joy, and permitting yourself to create small moments (think ad hoc dance party in the kitchen with wooden spoons or rock paper scissors or drawing on the back of the napkin contents with your kids) is where the power lies. It is impossible to curate joy 24/7, but it is possible to believe that joy can happen at any time. Permit yourself to create joy (big and small ways) and go.

Perspective

I think we start out in the world happy and excited little minds that just want to explore, be entertained, and learn. We are wholesomely optimistic but then life happens, and it gets in the way of happiness. Responsibilities and stressors get bigger, and all of the things we took for granted (such as joy) are replaced with a bit of stress, burnout, anxiety, fear, and anger, and all of a sudden we are a 30-something-year-old mom with a busy career, a spouse, kids, and a mountain of laundry...and dishes...and bills...and the invisible weight of it all becomes heavy, chaotic, and sometimes out of our control altogether.

There is a great visual by Stephen Covey called the Circle of Influence (sometimes known as the Circle of Control) that says, "Focus your energy and attention where it counts, on the things over which you have influence over. As you focus on things within your Circle of Influence, it will expand."

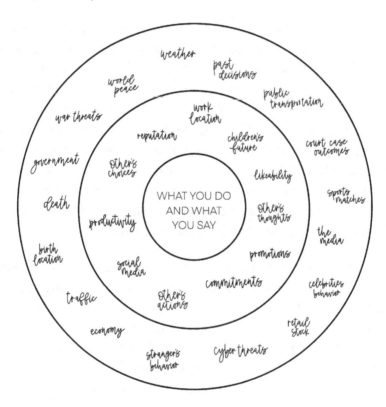

Brilliant, right?! You can only control you—what you do and what you say. Therefore, anything outside of that can only be influenced, and in many cases, you will not be able to affect it at all.

My husband and I have this made-up principle called the "do nothing or do something" principle, where we ask each other (when something challenging happens, or we are upset, or we get angry) whether we want to do anything about it or be ok with doing nothing. The key here is to be intentional with our decisions (what we do and say). I cannot control traffic, but I can do nothing and be upset or I can affect the moment by having a dance party in the car...Or when I feel the burn of driving my kids back and forth to practice (who decided that kids should practice 2-3 times a week anyway?!); what a great way to catch up on some audio books as I play chauffeur.

At work, I had an employee barge into my office frustrated about an update to the PTO (paid time off) policy. Since we had talked about the Circle of Influence before, I asked her, "What do you want to do? Nothing or something?" Her response was, "Something! Can I get on the committee that decided this policy?" In that moment, I was very proud of her because she had realized that if she did nothing, she would continue to be frustrated and angry. She also realized that she had options on the "something" she could do part. After 3 years, the policy had not changed, but when I asked her about the experience, she said she was glad she was in control of her response to the moment.

When the going gets tough, it's up to you to shape your perspective and to be in control of what you do and say. Being able to identify (in those crazy moments where you are ready to pull your hair out, or put on jammies and call it a day) that the thing you are upset about, or feel pressure from, is actually out of your control and decide how you want to respond in that moment. Joy is a process of being in a moment, realizing that much of it might be out of your control and maybe less than ideal, and then saying, "But does it have to stay negative or can I make this moment more enjoyable?"

I'm here to tell you that being best friends with joy takes work (yes, I like to think of her as a real person who is by my side). It's mental warfare to wake up and decide to let joy be in charge instead of letting every other emotion win. But I am also here to tell you that we don't have time for our negative emotions to be the boss...joy should be the boss via awareness and mindset shifting! If we let negative thoughts control our brains, we are giving away our experiences, moments, and memories.

If I am having a bad day (like the time I drove to the wrong client location or when I was passed up for a promotion), I have a rule where I permit myself to have that emotion (fear, anger, or sadness) for some time (I usually set a timer or mark it on my calendar) and then after the allotted time, I have to let it go and ask myself, what would make this moment a little bit more enjoyable? I come up with reasons why joy should be in charge instead of that other emotion and I have gotten into the rhythm where my brain knows what to do without thinking, much like tying my shoe...muscle memory.

Joy Through it All

Sometimes terrible situations help you see what is important more clearly. In 2016, my husband and I realized that we were no longer in the right place to raise our family. We were living in Milwaukee, WI (still love that city for the music, food, and sports!), but did not love our jobs, and we were 4-5 hours away from our immediate family. Many of our weekends were spent traveling back for special occasions or just to visit. 5-hour rides with toddlers got old quickly! So we started to make plans to sell our house (since the market was hot) and thought we would live in a rental house for a year or so as we took the next steps in making our plan to find jobs and move back to Iowa.

When our house sold in a day and we were able to rent a cute duplex (100-year-old creamy city brick house) just a few blocks from our house, we thought this was going to be great! We rented a U-Haul and moved on a sunny Thursday afternoon, and the next day, we signed the paperwork for selling our house. That Thursday and part of Friday were long days, but once everything was inside the duplex, we felt a sense of relief and were excited to see our plan taking shape. The kids also seemed to love the new duplex, as it had plenty of space to roam.

Before planning the move and sale of our house, some of our closest friends had already invited us to their bachelor and bachelorette parties in Minnesota, and even though we were exhausted from moving, we made the trip that Friday afternoon, handing off the kids to grandparents! We had a great weekend and Sunday night we returned home to our duplex, where all of our boxes were still scattered everywhere. Monday I went to work, thinking to myself, "Why didn't you take a few days off to unpack?" That night I spent time unpacking the kitchen so we could now cook meals for the kids and told myself I would be able to make progress on putting things away the following weekend.

On Tuesday, July 11th, our wedding anniversary, I went to work again wishing I had taken time off to unpack. Mid-morning a toilet handle (the silver cylinder-looking kind) was accidentally pulled off a toilet in our clinic and we had a good-sized flood on our hands! I was working at a healthcare clinic at the time and it was located on the 6th floor of a very large square building. When the handle was pulled off, water started seeping across the floor and down into the other clinics below us, it was a disaster, literally!

I spent most of the day tromping through water and playing crisis manager, redirecting patients to different areas of our clinic, helping maintenance clean up the mess, and working with facilities on making sure things would be cleaned and "okayed" for patients to be in that space. I went home even more exhausted than I was from moving and a really fun weekend, but happy...thinking about how we were now living in our duplex and our old house had been sold. I got home around 6 pm and the very tall stacks of boxes were still everywhere, and my kids were having a blast playing tag and hide and seek throughout the house. I told my husband we should move all MY boxes upstairs to the third floor so they were out of the way (and the kids would not have any box collapse injuries). Though we were both tired, we agreed to move everything, knowing we would reward ourselves (because this day was also our wedding anniversary) with wine and pizza to end the night.

Around 9:00 pm we toasted to each other with a box of pizza and wine in two plastic cups! We went to bed that night feeling accomplished! Around 3:00 AM, we woke up to pouring rain and a huge boom that sounded like a bomb had just hit. We immediately looked out the window to see if an electrical box had been struck. We could not really see anything due to the wind and rain, and when we went to turn on the bedroom light, we noticed that the overhead light would not turn on but the hall night light was still working. My husband said he would flip the breaker and I told him I would check upstairs on the 3rd floor to see if anything was going on up there. Maybe a bunch of boxes had tipped because the boom had been so loud above us!

I got to the third floor and it smelled different, I could not describe the smell, but it was like the smell of burnt hair, definitely not a smoky smell. I came back to the main floor to wait for him to flip the breaker, and then all of a sudden the outlets started buzzing. I called him on my cell and told him to shut that off, that something was up with the electricity. He came back up and we both looked at each other wondering if we should call the fire department and have them take a look. Our kids, who were also awake due to the big boom, were peeking out of their bedroom doors. We ultimately decided to call the fire department and boy am I glad we did!

I put the kids in the van in the pouring rain and my husband met one slightly annoyed fire fighter to have him do a quick check. A couple more fire trucks pulled up and idled out front of our house. My kids, fully awake and entertained by the situation, were loving the flashing lights and watching the firemen standing right near the van. All of a sudden though, the firemen started running back to the trucks to pull ladders, hoses, and axes out. I was like...this is real...like real-real. I pulled around the block so my kids would not see any of what happened next, which ended up being a pretty big fire.

Thankfully, I had an aunt and uncle in Milwaukee, so the kids and I left my husband at the house and drove to their house. The kids went back to sleep for a few hours and I ran to Walmart (thank goodness I grabbed my purse on the way out of the house) to grab some fresh clothes for the kids, and then dropped them off at daycare like nothing had happened. As far as they knew, the firemen just made sure the house was safe. As I drove up to the duplex, everything looked pretty good, that's a good sign I thought, but what I would find out shortly after was that everything was not good, not good at all.

My husband, whom I had not spoken to yet besides a few short text messages, met me at the door (both of us were still in our pajamas). We had a moment of "Holy s***, what just happened?" Then he says to me, "Remember last night when we moved all your stuff upstairs." Immediately, it dawned on me that he meant my belongings were what had burned. I could not believe the amount of insulation that had fallen from the ceilings due to the fire hose water. Window dormers had been kicked in and there was a large hole in the roof. The third floor had 3 inches of sludge covering the floor and everything was either burned or looked like it had exploded because the pressure of the fire hoses was so intense. I remember the fire inspector asking me what company we wanted to use to board up the windows and I looked at him like he was speaking German...there were so many things to process. Now that we were no longer homeowners, we also had a landlord to loop into the conversation.

That morning everything in our world stopped. We had so much to figure out. Where to live, how to get our stuff sorted and cleaned, and what our insurance would cover. It was chaos. In my mind, the first order of business was to find a place to live. So after handing our kids and a garbage sack of their wet clothes off to grandparents, who had started driving towards Milwaukee the minute they heard about the fire, I drove down the street to a few apartment buildings to see if they had anything for rent. Thankfully a two-bedroom was available on Friday – three days from now. Now all we had to figure out was how to furnish the said apartment and deal with the mess of the burnt house.

My husband and I had not eaten in who knows how many hours, so we decided to grab food and a drink at a local pub. Ironically, it was a sunny late afternoon and so we sat outside rehashing what had just happened, saying things like... "I can't believe it...can you believe it?" Then shifting our attention to the task at hand, of signing the lease for the apartment and renting furniture...who knew you could rent an entire apartment with furnishings (pots, pans, towels, dishes)? They bring you everything! I commented as we got up from the table—still smelling like burnt marshmallows—and said... "This next few months will be a wild ride, we should try to make the experience of living without all of our belongings and in a temporary place fun for the kids." In a very somber moment, we decided that joy was a choice.

The kids stayed with their grandparents for close to a week, which gave us time to prepare. We worked with our insurance carrier to catalog the items that burned and sort through the rubble. Anything salvageable was sent to a cleaning facility where it would spend the next 90 days. A big dumpster was set up outside the duplex for anything that was ruined, along with all that icky sludge. We took possession of the apartment and pretended we were camping. I went to the store and bought a few of their favorite games and toys so the apartment felt like home and kids from their school donated toys too. Kids are so resilient! When they arrived at our new place, they were excited to be "camping" and didn't seem one bit bothered by our less-than-ideal situation.

Just about the time you think you have it all together, or you think you have a joyful experience planned, life throws you a curveball and you are blown off track or told to take a timeout. It might be a natural disaster, a sick child, an ailing parent, or a work commitment that means you can no longer attend the game you were planning to attend, execute the beautifully created meal/date night, or travel to the amazing place. That is how life rolls, I wish I had some magic bullet to tell you that these moments will not occur, but alas, I do not.

In the past six months, we had been talking about moving back to Iowa and creating more joy, and I believe it was this situation that burned the idea into our minds (pun intended) that joy is our job...because the world was certainly not creating joy for us at that moment, ha! So, it was up to us, we would have to do it ourselves, and most certainly make joy through it all because we never know what is coming our way. Life is not perfect and pretty and neither is joy.

Sometimes when I am having a crappy day, I imagine joy as a friend. You can still have friends on crappy days, right?! And she is someone that shows up at the very right moment with a bottle of wine and says, "Did you forget about me? I am still here! No matter the weather, stage of my life, or what is happening to you, I can still drop by from time to time! Because YOU deserve it."

Season of Life

In between the sticky fingers, rubbing my kids' backs when they are sick, sprinting toward work and life deadlines, and trying to be a good partner to my husband, I try not to let myself push joy into the future. It used to be that "once" my kids are sleeping through the night, or "once" my work calms down, or "once" summer break comes...then I will focus on joy. I realized that the season of life (yes, the <u>amount</u> of joy you can have sometimes makes a difference), should not negate joy fully.

But Lisa, I have so much responsibility to accomplish things first ... really earn my joy, right? Yes, but is tomorrow truly guaranteed?! And will there always be another thing after the thing to accomplish? For example, we thought that once we finished college, we would get a job and it would be great. Then after getting the jobs and settling into a townhome, we got married. Of course, after we were married, then we would have fun, but after we got married, we were ready to have kids, and after that a car, and after that a senior-level title, and after that a better house...you get the picture. There is never a perfect time for joy because it's supposed to be woven throughout. Without it, your mental health suffers, your relationships suffer, and people become bitter and frustrated, unhopeful, unhelpful, and at the very least, unpleasant to be around. There is a cost to not having joy and the stakes are high.

I found that there are small things I can do that make a big impact. For example, leaving a post-it note for my kids in unexpected places, looking up a joke or a riddle to tell them in passing, and just being present (when they want to show me their trick for the billionth time) go a long way. Sometimes my husband and I do a "swap." The other night I sat and watched my kids play volleyball in the yard (smiling and nodding and cheering) while my husband trimmed the grass nearby. When he was done, we swapped and I weeded the garden while he refereed the volleyball match. Joy is about those tiny micro-moments that pass through each day.

I'll Have Joy Later?

After leading a team for close to five years, I was having coffee at Starbucks with a very high-ranking leader within our 40,000-person organization. I considered her a mentor and every so often we would get together to talk about my goals and aspirations, and she would advise me on how to handle any difficulties or challenges I was facing. I don't know how we landed on it, but the question of her retirement came up. She said, "Many people wonder when I will retire, but I always think to myself, what in the world would I do with my time if I retired?"

It was a bit surreal to hear her say this and her answer made me wonder if she had hobbies or things she liked to do outside of work. There was probably a very good chance that she did not because her job was 24/7 and incredibly stressful. She had spent 40+ years saving countless lives and spearheading some amazing work, leaving her with little time for other things.

Our conversation continued and she gave me great advice on how to deal with a couple of tricky situations I was experiencing with my team and another department. I was grateful for her guidance and wisdom, but my mind kept drifting back to the statement, "What in the world would I do with my time?" For the three years I had known this leader, I wanted to be JUST like her when I grew up. She was the one I was modeling my work behavior after and now I was reconsidering how my future work path might shape up. A small part of me was having a panic attack because I wanted to have things that light me up outside of work. Things I cannot wait to go and do, go be, or even go see. I made a micro decision at that moment to have both; work and hobbies that I could take with me into retirement. A week later I joined a Zumba class.

Don't Need More Joy

I once had a woman stand up to ask a question during a joy at work session, (we were just getting ready to brainstorm some joy at work ideas) in a snarky tone, "Lisa, what if you already have enough joy?" She looked over to her friend at that same table and they both snickered. I stood at the front of the room (honestly feeling flushed and a little frustrated) and responded, "Do you have a lot of joy?" She smiled and said, "Yes, I do." And I responded, "Good. I think you will be a great teacher of joy to others. I would love for you to serve as a joy expert during this next activity, and share some examples of how you create joy for yourself and others, family, or friends." Her smile dropped slightly, I think she could feel my authentic desire to spread joy, and she said thank you into the microphone and sat down. Things don't always need fixing in our lives, don't fix what is not broken. But rather share what is going well and how you are making it happen (it's the process, not the outcome).

There is an award ceremony in my town called the Sages Over 70, and the celebration is to honor people who are over 70 and have made the city a better place to live through their civic and business leadership, mentorship endeavors, and community advocacy. This past year I heard that one of the honorees stood up and said, "I'd like to think that instead of passing my torch to the next generation, I can use my torch to light those around me so we can all burn bright."

Yes, so much yes!

Definition of Joy

What counts as joy? Are there any parameters or a specific definition? Is joy the same thing as happiness? These are the questions I talk about in my keynotes and workshops. We wrestle with these concepts and the first time I got the question, "Are there specific parameters I should follow when creating joy?" I said I don't have any specific parameters in mind, just that joy should be something that makes your life better, brighter, and a little more fun. I also went home that night and searched the dictionary to see if it could bring forth any specific parameters. This is the definition hunt (or slight rabbit hole) that I went on:

The definition of joy is a feeling of great <u>pleasure</u> and <u>happiness</u>.

> The definition of pleasure is a feeling of happy satisfaction and <u>enjoyment</u>.

> The definition of happiness is an emotional state characterized by feelings of joy, <u>satisfaction</u>, contentment, and fulfillment.

> > The definition of enjoyment is the state or process of taking pleasure in something.

> > The definition of satisfaction is the fulfillment of one's wishes, expectations, or needs, or the pleasure derived from this.

This is where I stopped. I spent a lot of time thinking about which parts of these definitions made the most sense for what I was trying to convey and I have decided that these definitions showcase and confirm that joy is a feeling (most often resulting from a mindset shift and/or the result of an action) that increases your happiness levels. More simply put, a feeling you get from shifting your mind or performing an activity (aka by completing a joy challenge or creating and executing on a joy calendar).

Throughout the remainder of this book, I want you to consider:

o The definition of joy that you currently carry and the things that you tell yourself related to joy.

o The barriers that stand in between you and joy, and whether or not you want to do something or nothing. If your gut says, "you could be having more joy," then I encourage you to follow that feeling and acknowledge that you might have to shift your thinking just a bit, to give yourself permission or a new perspective. If after reading, you realize that you are exactly where you want to be, that is great too!

I hope you feel affirmed (or inspired) in the way you are approaching joy and that you also grab some joy ideas.

PART 2

Barriers to Joy

At the end of each barrier you will find inspirational joy drawings from
Alaina (9 years old) and Sawyer (11 years old)

The Things That Get in the Way

There is an arcade near our house that our kids love to go to. When you walk in, the noise and visual stimulation are stifling, endless beeping, ringing, and excited shouting. The bar near the back serves kiddie and adult slushies, snacks, and of course they sell candy and more candy. There are games like connect four basketball and Mario racing, plus a bunch of classic games like skee ball, pinball, and down the clown. I admit, I am a sucker for the classic games because they remind me of my childhood and the feeling of being lost in the moment. The only difference is that the machines no longer spit out red paper tickets, but rather you use a plastic card that keeps track of your tickets electronically...how the times have changed!

The one game that eerily reminds me of being an adult though, is Pac-Man. Each dot reminds me of a task on my to-do list waiting to be completed, and they are never-ending (sorry in advance if I am forever ruining this game for you)! You just eat and eat and eat until you pass the level, only to be given a reward of a new level with even more dots! The colored Ghosts seem a lot like each challenge in life, there are so many of them popping up randomly and they can change directions or speed up at any moment... why do there have to be so many?!

Though I would love to rid my days of the dots and ghosts, those pesky little barriers to all things joy-related, I have realized that they are here to stay (among all the kicking and screaming that I want to do) and there are only two options: let them consume me or battle on.

The Things We Tell Ourselves

Our brains are beyond powerful in convincing us that things either are or they are not (joyful or not), but I am here to tell you that our brains are sometimes wrong...

I had a philosophy professor who frequently made us draw numbers from a bucket for philosophical debates. The students who drew a one were to be FOR the selected idea and the students who drew a two were AGAINST. On one particular day, the topic was whether two things in the world can be true at once. I will never forget when one student stood up, walked to the front of the room, and said, "All I know is that I know nothing," and sat down (a great Socrates quote, isn't it?). Another student raised their hand and said, "If an animal is a cat, the same animal cannot be not a cat." The law of noncontradiction; also a good one! We could have sat there all day debating the nuances of each angle, but I left firmly believing that two things can be true at once because as the debate waged on that day, I was having two very opposite feelings. My cousin Erin passed away just a few months before that (remember the bright and fun 22-year-old I mentioned earlier?). I was, at that very moment, sad about her death (sometimes struggling to study in the library because my mind would wander to her) and yet happy to be a semester deep into my college career learning and experiencing and debating my way through the world. How was it that two things could be happening at once?

In this next portion of this book, we are going to tackle the things that get in the way of joy (kids, work, family, stress, money, etc.) and wrestle with the things we tell ourselves as to why joy just is not possible. Our brains are beyond powerful in convincing us that things either are or they are not (joyful or not), but I am here to tell you that our brains are sometimes wrong because we can be busy and joyful, have no money to our name and be joyful, overrun with housework and kids and yet still be joyful.

We will look at each barrier individually and the goal will be to walk through the things we tell ourselves, the obstacles, and provide some ideas on how to create joy despite the challenges we face. Know that you are not alone in your quest for joy and that millions of people know what it feels like to be overwhelmed, underappreciated, and burned out. Also, know that some of the joy ideas that I introduce are quick and easy so that they actually fit into our lives. I am sorry, Pinterest moms who love a perfectly curated experience with a photo op at the end, this is not that. This is meant to be an in-motion "how to guide."

Some of the barriers may resonate with you deeply and others may not. Know that this part of the book is intended for you to pick and choose, based on your want or need, life season or circumstances. I try to jam-pack each barrier with joy ideas and you may find those helpful for day-to-day.

Your job will be to take the ideas and strategies I give you and make them your own. I wish we were in the same room to dive deeper, but instead, I will give you stories and ideas that you can customize and adjust to work for your life.

This is how each barrier will be organized:

o **Justification** - the things that we tell ourselves on why we cannot have more joy (trust me, I do this too).

o **Obstacles** – the permission and perspective we need to overcome. I put the new way of thinking in bold.

o **Your Turn** – List out ideas to add to your Joy Calendar. You should walk away from this book with a shifted mindset and actionable ideas to create more joy. **Joy List Ideas** – I have not fully introduced this concept yet (See Part 3 of this book), but I want you to walk away with specific activities that you can do.

I'm Busy

Busy

Joy can be a part of the "busy."

Justification – what we tell ourselves.

Guilty as charged. If you believe that your biggest barrier to joy is that you are busy, know that you are not alone. Just last week I counted five of my friends who mentioned how busy they felt and how they were trying to "make it all work" with schedules, work, and kids. I have bad news and good news. The bad news is that you will continue to be busy, always. You will be personally busy and if not that, you will be professionally busy, or both! You will be so busy sometimes that you will be unable to imagine anything else fitting into your schedule and your brain will convince you that is just the way it is. But the good news is that your brain is wrong because as we know from earlier in this book, two things can be true at once. You can be busy, and the busy can be filled with a bit of joy.

Obstacles – the permission and perspective we need to overcome.

I used to wear my busyness as a badge of honor and it pains me to think about it because I emphasized the wrong thing. We all have responsibilities and things needing attention. Even as I sit here typing this, I look around my kitchen and can see at least three or four things that need tending to — dishes, my to-do list, and crumbs on the counter from my kids' morning bagel. What I now tell myself when I think about all my busyness is that joy can be a part of the "busy." When I get up to take care of the dishes (assuming no one is home), I make myself turn on my favorite podcast or music to lighten my mood. When I was working on sweeping up the crumbs again (the third time today), I did the same thing.

To combat our busyness, my husband and I have come up with a system for calling out the other person for claiming to be too busy. If one of us mentions that we are too busy or that we are working too much, the other person will turn and with raised eyebrows say (in their best announcer voice), "It sounds like someone needs to add some more joy!" This usually makes us laugh and certainly breaks the cycle. Having a signal or phrase has been a helpful way to remind the other person that they have a choice in their joy.

Your Turn

If you catch yourself saying, "I am busy, burned out, overwhelmed, or things are chaotic," that is a signal you need more joy in your life ASAP. Here are a few strategies and ideas.

Create a "things to do" List

I remember the third year of my husband's residency program, we had just had our second child, a baby girl, and our blonde haired blue glasses wearing son was a busy 2.5-year-old toddler who loved to run, jump, and climb everything! My husband's schedule was "lighter" (if that is possible for a resident physician who could work 100 or so hours a week) due to reduced paternity leave for our daughter, and we decided that though we did not HAVE time for joy with our busy little family, we needed to make time. This would be one of our last summers living in Milwaukee before we were scheduled to move back to Iowa, so why should we not enjoy it? Summers in Wisconsin are absolutely beautiful, probably the only reason why people put up with the very cold and snowy winters in this part of the country (I am mostly kidding), so in preparation for our last months by the lake, I got to work.

I printed off list after list of "things to do in Milwaukee" and started to piece together a summer filled with joy, or as much as I thought we could have with a newborn and toddler! Some of our favorites include: Riding the dollar trolley, a picnic at the beach, Brewer's game to eat a giant bag of popcorn and watch the "big TV" as my son called it (he had no idea the game was going on right below him), trips to parks, restaurants, ice cream places, flying kites down at the lagoon, paddle boating, and more. Even though we were more sleep-deprived than ever and going on fumes, these were some of our best Milwaukee memories. I am thankful for the memories and commitment to being in the moment. It's amazing what can happen when you put your mind to it!

Though our summer in Milwaukee ended, we found that having a list of things to do at the ready was the best way to increase the odds that joy would happen. Have you ever gotten to a Friday date night without a restaurant reservation and done the classic, "where do you want to eat? I don't know, where do you want to eat?" You spend almost as much time making a plan as the actual activity. You need a joy list.

Be a Tourist in Your Town

The evolution of our "things to do list" has inspired us to occasionally be a tourist in our town, wherever we live, and even in the nearby places we visit. If we have a free afternoon or are feeling like we need to spice things up, we go and do things that our town is known for, or try all the "bests" in town (best ice cream, best coffee, best park). We also visit the places we haven't been to and permit ourselves to go back to some of our favorites. Three of our favorite things to visit are:

- Best Restaurant(s)
- Historical Landmark(s)
- Unique Photo op(s)

A few other ideas from my Joy Calendar are to take a photo at the highest point in town, eat each of the different genres of food (Mexican, Thai, Italian, French, Greek, Indian, Chinese, etc), have a picnic on a beach (get creative if you don't live by a big body of water), visit a museum, take a walking tour, go to an open mic night, and find a new favorite brunch spot.

Create Joy During Meals

One of our favorite "too busy for anything else" activities is to create joy during meals. We often plan themed meals or desserts. One summer we had pancake parties, grilled cheese parties, and fajita parties for our friends and neighbors. It was a great way to gather and feed 15 starving kids with little cleanup. Other times we change things up and eat on a blanket on the floor (dinner picnic) or eat out on the patio.

We have been known to listen to music, tell jokes, or drink our water out of fancy glasses with straws, taking turns toasting each other. Other times we will open our box of conversation topics we got on Amazon and fill the time with good old-fashioned visiting, kids do say the darndest things, don't they? We talk about the highs and lows of our day, the most surprising thing that happened that day, and the most interesting thing that happened. We vote on who had the most surprising thing happen to them and sometimes we make up stories (each person adding a sentence to the last person's sentence).

Bringing a little fun to our meals has brought great joy to our family and is a great way to squeeze some joy into our day. We have also gotten creative with meal joy because sometimes we eat on the go. Make your meal times count, whether you are officially sitting at a table together or not. Cheers!

Create Quick Joy (Fridays at 4:30 PM)

My neighbors and I have a standing 4:30 pm on Friday front porch drink date (because a lot of us work from home or own businesses), meaning whoever is available when a text goes out around 3 pm should join. It's not always the same group of people that attend, and we oftentimes don't have much time to devote, but we squeeze it in before the demand of the weekend activities and obligations begin because we know how important it is to curate friend joy (I think of it as a joy refill for my week). This is one of my favorite times of the week because I get to catch up on their lives, have a good laugh, and enjoy a quick guilt-free drink. Usually, I'm home by 5:30 pm recharged and ready to be on mom and wife duty!

A Quick Walk

Are you taking time to move? Another favorite thing I like to do is take a quick walk during lunch or when I need to get up from my desk. I work from home and if left unattended, I might never remember to get up and stretch or walk around, so I set reminders to myself to get up and move. We have a pond nearby and when the weather is nice I walk around it. I now have it down to a science...it takes me 12 minutes to make one loop and that is the perfect amount of time for a chapter in my audiobook or a quick catch-up phone call with family or friends. "Hi Mom, I've only got about ten minutes, but I wanted to catch up!" Those 12 quick minutes do more for my soul than I can express and I feel healthier and happier because of it. Youtube also has some great 10-minute office workout videos.

Mini Day dates

My husband's schedule and mine don't allow for a weekly date night due to our kids' sports and activities, but I am always looking a week or two ahead to see where there is an opening in our schedule to squeeze in a mini-date. I have a rotation of activities that take less than one hour and some of them include things at home and others do not.

For example, on Wednesday, Thursday, and Friday, my husband and I both work from home. He works from 6 am - 3 pm on those days and it has been great for us to go on a date (even from home) or pretend to "be on a date" from home from 3-4 pm. Our kids walk home from school and usually pony up to the island counter for a snack. Since their sports activities don't start for a few hours, this time is perfect for me and my husband to sit on the porch and talk, or go grab coffee together. We announce to our kids that we are officially on a date and they have grown accustomed to it. Though it's not a "normal" time of day, it is the perfect time for a date...Whoever said you cannot have a "day date"?! I also find that when we are feeling "too busy", a little joy takes just a bit of strain out of our relationship, almost like a pressure release.

Taking advantage of the things we already do

Sometimes people feel like they cannot have joy because they already have too much on their plate, and if they add one more thing to their day, it will be the straw that breaks the camel's back. I believe there is merit to this statement, but again I remind you that two things can be true. There can be a lot on your plate and you can create more joy inside of or in addition to what you have going on now. Take out your calendar and think about what you do pretty regularly, whether it's meals or laundry or cleaning the kitchen, and say to yourself, how do I infuse joy in the things I'm already doing so my mental to-do list does not get bigger, and no activities are added? You may want to say to yourself, "If I'm going to have a lot of things on my plate anyway, why not make one of them enjoyable?" We don't want everything in our life to feel like eating broccoli or exercising, right?

I have heard people say that you should make your bed right when you wake up because then you have already accomplished one thing before your day has even begun. You can do the same thing with joy. Take the 5 minutes when you first wake up, whether it's to enjoy a warm cup of coffee, a few minutes to yourself to stretch, or journal. For me, sometimes it's just laying in bed scrolling on my phone before I wake the kids up (naughty little habit). You already have things on your plate, so make them a little joyful.

Joy List Ideas

- Create a things-to-do list – it could be a list of things to do in your town, things to do on a rainy day, or things to try
- Be a tourist in your hometown
- Create more joy at meals
- Spice it up – create themes for your days, food, and parties
- Keep movin' – create small bursts of movement
- Use the in-between time – squeeze in a 10-minute joy activity
- Day Dates – with your partner or self!

Kid Joy Ideas

When asked what joy ideas they might have for this obstacle, my daughter Alaina (9 years old) and her friend Sawyer (11 years old) came up with these!

Too Tired

Justification - what we tell ourselves.

The barrier of being too tired is challenging because I think we will always be tired on some level (insert season of life or circumstance), it's a moving target. There will be times when you just cannot function without a little rest, and when that happens, you should take some time to recharge (even if it is a 15-minute power nap or Yoga Nidra, one of my favorites). Second, consider making the time that you are awake a little more joyful (6:30 – 10:10 pm for me). Pick joy activities that require <u>very little</u> extra brain space or physical energy, and think of joy as bite-sized morsels of joy in your already "in motion" day.

Obstacles – the permission and perspective we need to overcome.

I read an article on CNBC about how we are tired of people telling us how tired they are (in this instance at work). After reading this bold statement, I looked around at the coffee shop I was at to see if anyone else felt the same shock I did after reading this...and then I laughed because of course, I was the only one reading the article (facepalm). Why did this statement make me so uncomfortable? And what were they suggesting people do instead? I read on.

The article went on to say that people should not tell others they are tired because it: shuts down the conversation, they might sound bored or lazy, or it shows they are not working smart. I thought about this for a moment regarding the barrier of being tired and how that can be a barrier to joy. Hmmmm, what if there is some merit there? I tried to put it in the context of how it might go for me.

If I am feeling tired and I mention how tired I am to friends, and because they hear me say this, I get fewer invites to get together. What if this means I come off as bored or lazy (or another emotion altogether like anxious or angry), which is not what I am trying to portray? And what if that means I am not being smart with my time? In essence, I might be letting the world happen to me, not the other way around. This made me think...is letting tiredness take the lead the way to go?

Now my goal in sharing this isn't to make us feel uneasy or shameful about the tiredness we feel, but rather for us to consider and reframe how we talk and think about being tired. If you and I were sitting at a coffee shop talking about joy, when asked how we are doing, I would want either of us to be the one to say, "I am tired lately, but having a blast along the way." Now, in this instance, I would still believe that I would get invited to the next friend event, concert, or camping trip, and seem like I'm the person who would be "up for a good time," to stay up late and dance the night away or tell great stories by the fire.

My husband is a night owl. His ideal schedule would be to sleep until noon and then stay up until 2 in the morning. Real life gets in the way of that because his job requires him to start work at 6 am. His true golden hours (the time when he is at his best) are not in the morning, but rather in the evening. My golden hours are opposite of his, I am a morning person...give me all the 7:30 – 11:30 am times!

If you are looking for an easy way to sneak in some joy, follow your golden hours. Find a short time when you are at your best and capitalize on those hours. I use that 7:00 – 7:30 AM time for self-joy and my husband uses 10:00 – 11:00 pm for his.

If you are sitting there thinking, *Lisa, that all sounds great, but my golden hours land smack dab in the middle of my work day*, try to time your break or lunch at that time. The goal here is not to redesign your schedule or become frustrated that life does not align quite right, but rather to identify a snippet of time where you can create joy. I once had an employee who knitted during her work break, and when she was not knitting, she was painting her nails. I thought it was silly at the time, but when I asked her why she did her hobbies at work, she said, "Well, life is too busy otherwise, this is when I can sneak it in." Smart woman!

Your Turn

Joy can come in 10 in 15-minute increments.

What if I told you that you only have 15 minutes to create more joy? Could you do it? That's what I recommend for those feeling tired. If you are tired, it means you probably also don't have a lot of time, which we already touched on in this book, so you must take advantage of the nooks and crannies in your day. Whether it's reading one chapter of a book, writing a card or letter to a friend, painting or drawing, knitting, phone photography, yoga, meditation, calligraphy, crossword puzzles, cloud watching or star gazing, Rubik's cube, or even dream up a new recipe to try, there is no such thing as silly 10-minute joy.

Neck Yoga

Getting my kids ready in the morning is stressful and most days I feel like a robot on repeat. Did you brush your teeth? Did you fill your water bottle? Do you have your school folder? But I often try to create a moment of music or laughter with the kids. I stand at the top of the stairs and play my (or their) favorite songs. When it's time to come downstairs, the kids sit at black bar stools along the island and eat their eggs and toast or cereal, and I grab my laptop and sit next to them (if not scrambling to get ready for a meeting, ha!).

I hold all of my stress in my neck and shoulders and have realized that stretching before the day kicks off brings great rewards and relief. So while they eat, I fire up a 13-minute long shoulder yoga video from YouTube. The video can be done sitting or standing, so I play referee and stretch the stress away, killing two birds with one stone!

Exchange Screen Time

My sister and I often keep each other updated on when it's time for a social media or screen time break. We have realized that we slip into the habit (because it's oh, so easy) of using technology as our "break" or joyful activity.

I encourage you to think about transitioning some of your screen time, whether it's social media, looking things up on the internet, or a different joy activity. Don't get me wrong, I love a good scroll on social media, but I also know that stealing 10 or 15 minutes of screen time for hands-on joy is a better return on investment. I've heard of people rewarding themselves a point for each non-tech hour, or even as a family setting a non-tech goal. Maybe if you give up 10 hours of screen time as a family, you get to do something fun. The book How to Break Up with Your Cell Phone by Catherine Price talks about how she started taking tech sabbaticals from Friday night to Saturday and how it changed her life. It has also done wonders for her family and ours! We are not as dedicated, but have been better about leaving our tech at home when we go and do fun things.

Capitalize on the times right before or after

One way we create quick joy is by taking advantage of the times right before or right after. One quick example for our family is we do some sharing right before bed. Sometimes it's sharing highs and lows, other times it is what we would do again or not do again, something funny or surprising. We also found a journal on amazon called Ikigai that allows us to reflect on what our greatest purpose in life should be. It has been fun to hear our kids' perspectives on the world.

Right after I wake up in the morning, I try to meditate or do yoga, enjoy a cup of coffee, or journal. I find that it's easier for me to fit it in that way and permit myself to have a few minutes of me time, otherwise, I feel the need to complete housework or tend to others.

Pair joy with another activity

I once heard a trick for people forgetting their lunch at home. They said to tie the act of bringing your lunch to another activity. The idea was that if you put your car key in your lunchbox and put that in the fridge, you will never forget your lunch because to leave your house, you need your key. I think this applies to joy; you can create efficient and effective joy if you tie it to something that already exists.

Maybe once a week you turn the planning of your meals for the week into a joy activity (who can come up with the most interesting meal idea) or maybe you listen to music while you fold laundry, or maybe listen to an audiobook while driving your kids around.

Carry joy around in your car

We carry around trivia questions in our car's middle console so we can have a quick trivia tournament while driving. We also have mad libs, word finds, and other car games printed and ready to go because you never know when you will have an extra five minutes.

1-hour joy challenge

One of my favorite joy activities is to avail myself one hour to think of things I can squeeze in, especially when I am tired. Whether it is to check another coffee shop off our list, take a bath and listen to an audiobook, or paint a picture, I find that 1 hour is a perfect amount of time for a joy recharge. It is also the perfect amount of time for creating joy with my kids. Sometimes we build box forts in the garage, kick a ball around in the yard, or play pretend hair salon or hotel, but one hour makes it seem doable. Not too long or too short.

The 1-hour joy categories I often reference when planning are:

- Things to do
- Things to see
- Things to eat

A few from my Joy Calendar: Walk and talk (phone or in person), paint by number, cook a meal I have never tried, read a book, send snail mail, get a massage, read, nap outside, create a family scavenger hunt.

Joy List Ideas

- Short Burst (15-minute joy)
- Exchange Screen Time
- Before/After joy
- Pair your joy

- Joy with kids
- Car joy
- 1-hour challenge

Kid Joy Ideas

When asked what joy ideas they might have for this obstacle, my daughter Alaina (9 years old) and her friend Sawyer (11 years old) came up with these!

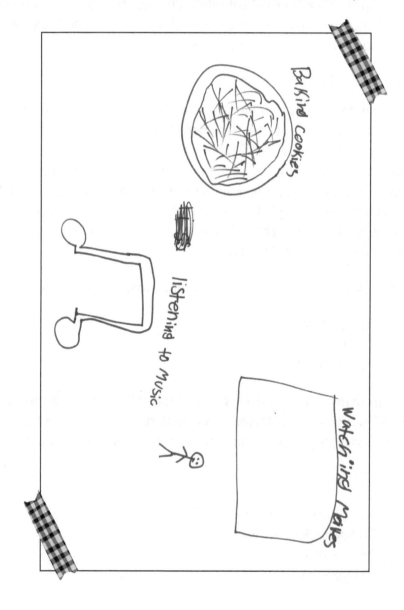

Money

Money

> *Joy costs (the amount of money you spend on joy) shift as your bank account does. No matter how much money you have, you can still have joy!*

Justification – what we tell ourselves.

I joined the workforce in 2008 at the height of the recession, there were very few jobs available and they did not pay well. The plan was to go to grad school on nights and weekends, and then work full-time during the day to support my boyfriend (now husband) and me while he went to medical school. I remember looking at our bank account some weeks, wondering if we were going to make the money stretch. Ironically, I also remember this time in our lives as some of the happiest. We were just as happy then as now and the money did not make or break the experiences we had. Our first home together was a townhome, and I got good at making my own art (spray paint is magic) and scouring Goodwill for decorations and household items. I found an old birdcage and that became the decoration in front of our 90s-looking fireplace. I grabbed paint samples from hardware stores and created art for the wall behind our couch. I even glued old belts to a canvas for more wall art.

We had a list of all the local restaurants with daily deals on our fridge. A burger joint near our house had dollar burgers one night of the week. You could get pizza deals and many other low-cost meal options on different days. Our kids love trying out all of our "good old time" meal deals. All this is to say that though a lot of things cost money, there are also a lot of things that don't. If you are struggling to find joy due to a lack of money, I encourage you to think about joy as a feeling and an action rather than something you have to pay for.

Obstacles - the permission and perspective we need to overcome.

I have memories from childhood when I visited neighbors, made cookies, and planted things with my dad in his garden. I have memories of being at my grandparents' house playing board games and making flower crowns. I have memories of playing outside in the hose, riding my bike, and gazing at the stars. I remember being a very poor, high school student who worked two jobs and played sports, who would scrape together quarters out of my dad's change jar to buy a McDonald's cheeseburger. If I think back to college, I remember sitting in dorm rooms with friends asking who had another dollar to order a pizza. What I realize now is that joy costs (the amount of money you spend on joy) shift as your bank account does. No matter how much money you have, you can still have joy!

Your Turn

Things Hiding in Plain Sight

One of the quickest things you can do to come up with joy ideas that don't cost a thing is to look around your house. You probably have board games, puzzles, crafts, old books, scrap paper, and things you have not done in ages. On different nights of the week, you may find us googling Mad Libs or trivia, printing coloring pages, or cutting pictures out of magazines or sale ads. Recently I taught my daughter how to make some of the bracelets I used to make with my friends and it made me reminisce about some of the times I spent with friends. We love to play family flashlight hide and seek, scavenger hunts, mazes that we create on paper, and cardboard box-building activities (forts, ice cream stands, race cars). The kids have a running list of movies they want to watch with Grandma and Papa on our refrigerator.

Just last week, when my kids were bouncing all over the house, we decided to build towers out of red solo cups and use them as bowling pins. The kids loved setting up the cup towers and we also decorated each cup with a Sharpie so we could tell which pins were which. So many things are hiding in plain sight, it just takes a bit of creative thinking to make it happen!

This coming summer, we planned to participate in Ragbrai, which is a six-day bike ride across our home state of Iowa (check it out if you are ever in this neck of the woods). We have bikes already and plan to pack sandwiches and snacks for the ride. We won't do the entire 6 days as that would require camping in different cities each night, but I am sure we will have some fun along the way. Check to see if there are events or activities in your area. I am always surprised at how many things are going on. Another favorite outdoor activity is in each city we visit, we try to take a food tour or a bike tour because there is nothing better than seeing a city or in this case, parts of a state from the seat of a bike.

If you are striking out on free joy with your kids, have them do some brainstorming! My son loves to play chess and my daughter is always up for painting my nails, makeup, or styling my hair. I ask them for joy ideas because their imagination is always in overdrive and they are not bogged down with responsibilities...they are fresh! You would be surprised how good kids can be at brainstorming free joy. Get them thinking about how they can contribute to their own joy and have a little fun along the way.

Adult Joy

Free or inexpensive joy ideas are not just for the kids! We have done staycations where we had a few days to just be lazy at home. We have done date nights where we cooked a pizza and watched a movie and told the kids to do the same in the basement. We have done themed vacations and road trips just because we needed more joy and played "What can you get for the money" in different cities across the world.

This past year, on the 4th of July, we invited friends over for a weekend of games and made Cuban sandwiches on the griddle. We had friend Olympics where we played patriotic games and gave out awards for the best dressed, even the best patriotic poem. On New Year's, we played minute-to-win-it games and had a signature cocktail contest. Recently we had a clean-out-your-freezer party with another family where the only rule was that the food you brought to dinner had to come from your freezer or fridge. We had quite the spread of food: pretzel bites, chicken wings, green beans, and coleslaw. Who is not looking to get rid of some of the food they have had forever and have been meaning to eat?

Create a Theme

One of the easiest things to do when brainstorming joy ideas is to come up with a theme. Whether it's food-related, sports- or hobby-related, or even something you completely make up, a theme always gets people excited to celebrate. If it's Mexican week, we have been known to do a pinata in the garage. And yes, you can make those from scratch. Cereal boxes work great and we have paired that with games, movies, and trivia.

We have done themed weeks or weekends, even silly ones, such as the one time we accidentally ordered way too many bananas on the online grocery app and needed a reason to eat them up. We made banana smoothies, pancakes, bread, and everything else under the sun we could think of. Our kids thought it was great!

Limit Technology

The one thing I will say about free joy is that we try to limit the amount of free joy that includes technology. Now, we are a lot like other families in that we get our fill of electronics, but when it comes to our joy calendars, we try to make that lower on the list. Google has some great "things to do lists" and I highly encourage printing them off and checking each one off when you have done them, so satisfying.

We also try to mix it up so that if we have had a couple of nights in a row with joy related to movies or shows, we switch it up. That does not mean we don't love a good binge of Wednesday Addams or other Disney week themed movies, it just means we know our joy can go stale if we do things over and over.

Boredom isn't a bad thing

Our kids know that boredom is not a bad thing. If they say they are bored, we will tell them that just means they will probably get a great idea very soon. That their mind will start searching for a good idea and will give them an idea of something to do soon. I would like to think that in the back of their mind, we are affirming the idea that joy is their job. That they have to come up with an idea and be in charge of their destiny.

There are times when the kids are whiny, but a few weeks ago I came into the kitchen and I heard my daughter telling her brother she was bored. My son said, in a voice that almost sounded like my husband's, "Well, that just means you are going to get an idea soon!" I burst out laughing and they both gave me a funny look. I told them I was proud of them for thinking about how to cure their boredom.

Helping Others

Two questions I ask my kids regularly are, what can you do to create more joy in the world and what can you do to create a positive impact? Creating impact brings joy. Whether it is making cards for nursing homes, sending letters to friends and family, leaving positive sidewalk chalk messages, or making care packages for those in need, my goal is to have them realize they can create joy for themselves, but also for others in very small but effective ways. The kids have commented that creating joy for others feels good and they are exactly right!

Good Conversation is Joy Too

Good conversation is joy too. Whether it is with friends or family, a good conversation is worth its weight in gold, and good conversations are very free. We have a couple of boxes of cards that have conversation starters on our living room coffee table and they have been a blast with our kids and even friends. Oftentimes, it feels like we are in a rut and there is nothing inspiring or new to talk about. Now I am a dreamer and always want to dream up the fun things we could do, but I know it is not a normal quality, so our conversation cards have come to the rescue many times.

As a family, we often say high and low at the dinner table. Tell me one amazing thing that happened today and one not-so-great thing. I changed up the questions I asked my kids to get better conversations because hearing some of the funny and interesting stories they have to tell is the absolute best. I even printed a list of questions to ask off the internet. And I tell you what, it has made a difference. Our conversations are more joyful and more interesting each day.

Joy List Ideas

- Board games, puzzles, crafts
- Mad Libs or trivia, printing coloring pages, or cutting pictures out of magazines or sale advertisements
- Freezer meal party or pantry party
- Minute to win it games
- Solo cup bowling
- Cardboard box house or fort building

Kid Joy Ideas

When asked what joy ideas they might have for this obstacle, my daughter Alaina (9 years old) and her friend Sawyer (11 years old) came up with these!

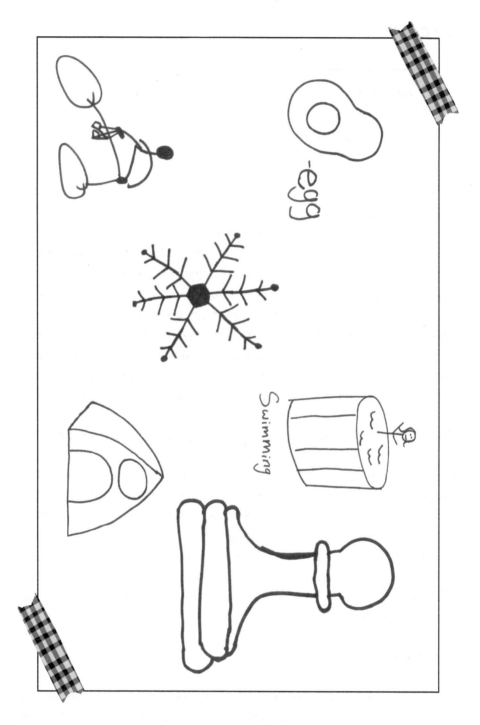

Not Creative

not creative

Some is better than none and perfect is a farce.

Justification – What we tell ourselves.

Some of my "not creative friends" have been able to develop amazing joy lists and calendars by doing a bit of looking online. If you are not creative or don't know where to start with joy ideas, the good news is that the internet and Pinterest can be great friends to you (be sure to pick some of the easy and quick ideas first)! I permit you to steal shamelessly! Sign up for mom newsletters and join mom groups and travel groups on social media that have ideas for family fun, vacations, and trips. Sometimes I don't have time to keep up with all the emails, but in a pinch, when I need a joy idea, they are there. I also think it's helpful to have ideas sent to me instead of me having to search around!

Obstacles - the permission and perspective we need to overcome.

Sometimes I feel like I need to be Instagram perfect and I do one of two things. I either go to crazy lengths to make it seem like I have it together or do nothing at all. I now tell myself that: some is better than none and perfect is a farce. A friend once said that the problem with people thinking they can't be a runner is that if you lace up your shoes and run 20 feet, you still get credit for being a runner. You do not need to create a perfect joy list and you certainly don't need to execute it perfectly because that would be impossible.

Your Turn

A few of our favorite unconventional joy ideas have included making sidewalk chalk stained glass pictures, playing hot potato with the painter's tape wad after removing it, making obstacle courses using painter's tape, glow-in-the-dark dance parties, throwing glow sticks in the pool to have a glow party, and blowing up tons of balloons to play with. One summer, I gave my kids our city catalog which listed every single park and they spent the entire summer checking them off their list. We called that summer our Park Adventure.

Traditions and Celebration

Many of our joy activities have inspired annual traditions or have sparked ideas for celebration. We always celebrate the first snow of the year as if it were a holiday. We have celebrated the first day we plant our garden, the first day of spring... If it even seems like it might be a good reason to celebrate, we do!

When we recently traveled with friends to California, it was their daughter's first time flying, so of course we needed to treat that as her Travel Birthday and eat cupcakes and sing to her as if it was her actual Birthday. I hope my kids get the idea that they don't have to wait for an official day or celebration to come to them to celebrate. They can celebrate any day of the year!

Steal shamelessly

I already said it, but I will say it again, steal shamelessly and then go reinvent and reengineer these ideas to adapt them specifically for you. Some of the things that might happen in small-town Iowa, like being on a farm and spending time playing in a creek, might look very different in an urban city apartment building. But Joy is not a stranger to any type of environment, she can be found around every corner or in my case, cornfield.

Joy List Ideas

- Find joy ideas online (i.e. mom newsletters, join mom groups and travel groups on social media)
- Create unconventional joy
- Create traditions and reasons to celebrate
- Park Adventure challenge - try out local parks

Kid Joy Ideas

When asked what joy ideas they might have for this obstacle, my daughter Alaina (9 years old) and her friend Sawyer (11 years old) came up with these!

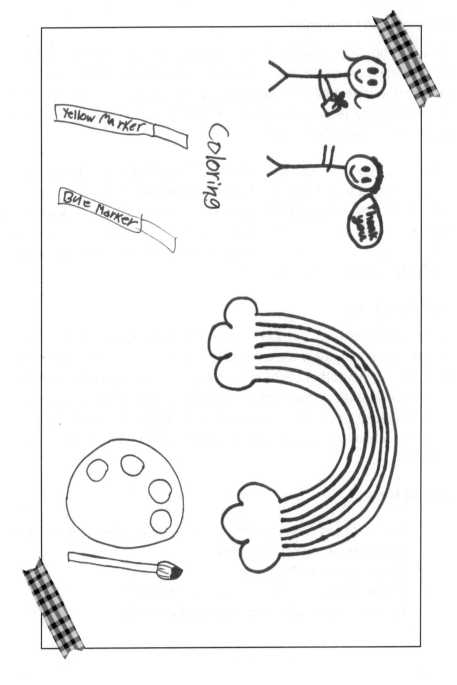

Going Through a Tough Time

Going Through a Tough Time

Don't wait for better days to create joy, they are not guaranteed.

Justification – What we tell ourselves.

I recently changed desk chairs, was sick with COVID for two weeks and lived on my couch, then followed it up by wearing terrible shoes to a wedding and found myself with a pretty intense back ache. It was a time full of excruciating pain where it felt best to stand or lay, nothing in between. My kids and husband waited patiently for my symptoms to dissipate, but I felt a little downtrodden about my inability to participate in normal day-to-day activities. Sound familiar?

If there is something negative, uncomfortable, or out of your control happening to you (or someone close to you) at this very moment, you are not alone. These moments need joy more than others. I have a note in my phone with joy ideas and some of them are perfect for a rainy day. During my back ache, joy looked like a movie in bed with my kids curled up next to me, a dip in the hot tub, playing a board game while sitting on a heating pad, and having my kids turn into my "restaurant helpers" by making me drinks or snacks and bringing them to me. My joy list was small but mighty!

Obstacles - the permission and perspective we need to overcome.

Similar to what I mentioned earlier, don't wait until you accomplish "the thing." Don't wait for better days to create joy, they are not guaranteed.

I have a dear friend who in her early 30s went through breast cancer right after the birth of her daughter. I cannot fully imagine what the experience was like, but as a bystander and friend, I know there was more pain than joy most days. When I asked her about finding joy during that crazy time (cancer and COVID), it was interesting to listen to her perspective because she talked more about mindset than anything else. It was very important to her that she stay positive for her husband and daughter. She came back to the idea that choosing joy is a choice. I asked her if she could email her list of joy ideas to share with you all and I share them with you now.

Joy List Ideas While Having Cancer

Her disclaimer: Keep in mind we have only had a toddler during COVID, so we did not go many places and most of our joy revolved around our daughter.

- Cooking breakfast - Our daughter loves to help cook breakfast on the weekends (mixing muffins, mixing pancakes, and beating the eggs). Sometimes we will even have breakfast for dinner.
- Pizza and movie nights – we have introduced her to a lot of Disney movies. We always try to cook a pizza and buy movie-size candy so each of us gets a different flavor.
- Car picnics - Over the summer, since we were not eating in restaurants, we would get carryout and have a "car picnic." Eat in the back of the car or tailgate of the truck.
- Drive-in Movies – we have thought about venturing over to a drive-in theater in the metro and filling the tailgate of the truck with blankets and pillows, but our daughter is just a little young for it since it has to start after dark and she is already in bed by then.
- Shopping at the Nursery or any outdoor place - we enjoyed taking her with us to the outdoor nursery to pick out plants for the house. Lots of room to run and she enjoyed climbing up and down the outdoor patio furniture too.
- Errands - we call it a mission or adventure which seems to make it more enjoyable for her.

Kid Joy Ideas

When asked what joy ideas they might have for this obstacle, my daughter Alaina (9 years old) and her friend Sawyer (11 years old) came up with these!

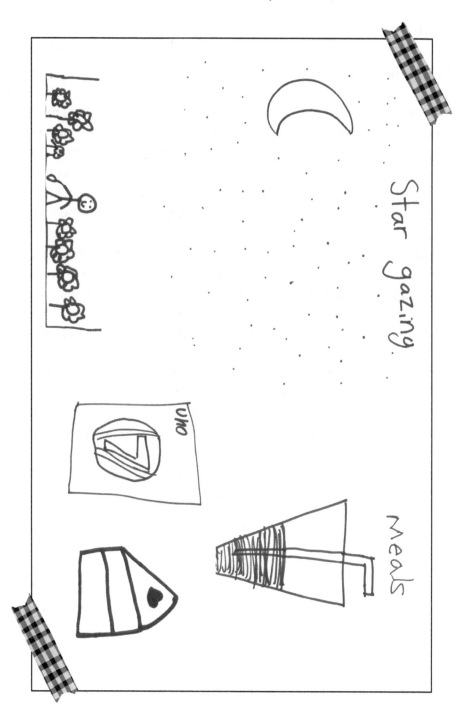

Work

Work

Work

Justification – what we tell ourselves.

I remember taking my first job and wanting to do the very best job that I possibly could. I was willing to do anything to make a good impression and for each of the projects and tasks I was given, I made sure to spend a little extra time on them at night. I would get up early and work while I ate breakfast to ensure that everything was as perfect as I could get it. I would get home from work, open my laptop and work some more. I would eat some dinner and do one final email check before crawling into bed. That was the cycle, day in and day out. I will tell you that on the one hand, this is a great way to get promoted and noticed by leaders in the organization. But what I did not realize is that working non-stop is also a great way to get more work assigned to me. The people that do a great job get rewarded with more work (said in a nice tone of voice).

I think it was in my third job out of college that I realized I was burning the candle at both ends. I was not overwhelmed, but I WAS saying no to a lot of things outside of work so I could keep running at a high level, that should have been a sign. My husband was working a lot too and without paying much attention, we had fallen into a bad habit of thinking that working non-stop was normal. This cycle of work, work, work, did not stop until an interaction with my boss.

I had worked all weekend on a project we were getting ready to bring to our team. I walked into his office Monday morning for my 1x1 meeting, ready to discuss. On Friday he had said he would do his part of the project and I needed his information to keep things moving. The conversation started like every other 1x1 I had had. He asked me how things were going and I took that opportunity to showcase the work I had done over the weekend. When I finished, I patiently waited for him to do two things: first, tell me I did a great job, and second, share what he had done over the weekend, his progress. I do think he told me good job, but I remember him skipping his update, moving on to another unrelated topic on our meeting agenda. I could not think straight. Why did he not give me an update? Had he not done anything over the weekend?

After a minute, I stopped him and said, "Can we go back for just a sec? How are things going for you on the project?" I think he knew what I was alluding to, though I was trying to say it in the most pleasant tone I could muster. He responded, "Since not much time has passed since Friday when we spoke, I haven't done anything about it yet." I was shocked. I am sure I had a goofy confused look on my face. He followed up with, "Lisa, work is work and home is home. I try very hard not to mix the two. There are very few times that I work at home because that is time I give to my family." I nodded as if I knew what the heck he was talking about. I got back to my office and rolled that over in my head.

On the one hand, I was so mad at him that I wanted to go back into his office and tell him he was not a team player and that he did not care enough about the project at hand. Thankfully I did not do that because things would have ended differently, and not in a good way. Instead, I stewed on it all week. I did not open up my computer when I went home that night, or the next morning, or the next. I was so mad still and I was determined (in my head) to prove that there would be no way for our team to function without extreme dedication.

I waited for the world to come crashing down, but it did not. Honestly, nobody even noticed that I was not cranking out a crazy amount of work. It was not until a few months later when someone said to me, "I noticed you weren't checking emails over the weekend, did you do something fun?" that I realized our team would be (and was) just fine. I was sad that I had spent years over-working without needing to, but I am thankful for that experience because it taught me that I can work appropriately hard (because I am still a hard worker) and also have joy.

I break my own rule on occasion and work on something during family time, but it's not the norm. I have also realized that, because I own my own business, I can shift my work time. I try to end my day (when I am not speaking or coaching) by 3:30 pm and then on Saturday and Sunday mornings before the family is awake, I make a cup of coffee and spend an hour catching up on emails and work. I have retrained my brain to say, Lisa, we don't need to do this task during family time. Why are you feeling this way? If I ever do have to work after hours, I try to infuse fun in the middle. Sometimes it's a popsicle or ice cream break with my kids or 20 minutes to go on a walk and stretch my shoulders. I have noticed great results in my mental health, physical health, and happiness health.

Joy is a choice and requires micro-bites of intention, action, and reflection. If you have a heart condition, you modify your diet, If you have an orthopedic injury, you get physical therapy.

Obstacles - the permission and perspective we need to overcome.

I want you to envision that today is the last day of your career. Whether you are a stay-at-home mom or a CEO, imagine that you are leaving your place of work (office, desk, or home) for the very last time. You have everything packed up and walk across the room and put your hand on the door handle, butterflies in your stomach. You are just about to open the door and before you turn the handle, out of the corner of your ear, you hear someone say, "They were really _____." What do you hope to hear? Take a moment to jot that down on a piece of paper. Maybe it's a word or a statement. Maybe it's a feeling or an accomplishment. Somewhere below the surface of what you just wrote, I hope there is a hint of joy in it.

On the last day of my career, I hope to hear that she worked hard and played hard! That she left the working world a little better than she found it.

If you have worked in the corporate world for any length of time, you are used to metrics and results. I spent a good portion of my career in healthcare before starting my own company, and let me tell you, we would measure everything! How sick you are, how much better you got, how fast we got you better. We kept track of the supplies we used, the time it took us to complete certain tasks, and even the conditions our patients had in relation to their age; if you could name it, we could measure it! Though it felt tedious, the experience of looking at cause and effect (inputs and outputs) and studying the details comes in handy when thinking about joy.

Joy is your legacy for yourself...and others.

Joy is a choice and requires micro-bites of intention, action, and reflection. If you have a heart condition, you modify your diet, If you have an orthopedic injury, you get physical therapy. There is an opportunity to shift focus to the outcome you desire and pair that with small changes (think a fun version for broccoli and exercise, ha). HOW I can bring joy to the forefront of my actions and activities and begin to track the outcomes? What will I see as a result? Am I seeing progress in having more joy? Less stress? Lower blood pressure? Better conversations? Better relationships? The benefits are endless!

Now you might be ready to give "metrics" a kick in the pants, but I would like you to note that when it comes to joy, there is a real return on investment (ROI) for the time and energy spent. Of course, there will be times when joy does not come to fruition, but your brain will thank you for your efforts anyway. The evidence will be your emotional health, your relationships with your friends, family, and co-workers, as well as the memories you create. In a way, joy is your legacy for yourself....and others.

Your Turn

The people in your life have a front-row seat. And you, whether you know it or not, are the permission giver (through your actions and words) to the ones you love for a lot of things. If they see you constantly working, you are sending a non-verbal signal (or permission) to them to do the same. If you are having all joy and no work, you are permitting that too. I hope my family sees that I am working hard and playing hard, I want them to feel like they have permission to do the same.

I was once at a work event where someone mentioned my joy calendar and how they tell their kids, "Do as I say, not as I do." They said they worked too much, probably drank too much caffeine and alcohol, and did not have the balance thing figured out. Their response made me sad and I spent the next 15 minutes encouraging (ok, trying to convince) them that they could get a little more balance, or at least a little more joy if they made it their focus. I hope they walked away with the idea that joy is their JOB.

During a conversation with a coaching client in the manufacturing industry, we were talking about what makes him stressed. He told me he had a heart attack two years ago and he is not doing that anymore, and that now very little stresses him out. He went on to say that there will always be more work and more things on the to-do list. He is right. There will always be more things to do and WE get to design and tinker with the level of stress, unhappiness, or joy in life.

Creating Joy at Work

My curiosity about whether I could create more joy at work started after our house fire. It happened to also be a time when I was not happy at work and so I thought *well, I'm creating joy outside of work, now I need to do the same here too.* I pulled my team together for a morning meeting and asked them to write down how to create more joy or fun at work (work hard AND play hard, right?). At first, I had only a handful of people turn in ideas, but as the weeks went on, I got a few more and a few more. Six months in, we created a social committee to be the executors of the joy Ideas. I was surprised by how creative they could be with a very low budget to come up with ideas ($20 budget per month). We did not term it a joy calendar, but looking back, it was.

Most of us will work close to 90,000 hours in our careers and that's a lot of hours to not have joy!

We started small with things that were already on the calendar: nationally recognized days of celebration (national donut day, coffee day) and holidays (office Easter egg hunt, Irish mad lib contest, and Holiday bingo via email). Then we started to get more creative, sports tailgates, "give back day" by making sandwiches for a homeless shelter, and guest speakers who would come in and share inspiration and knowledge. We had people bring in photos from when they were a baby or at prom and everyone guessed who was who. These tiny tiny little slices of our day, where our brains were thinking about something other than work, created more laughter and better collaboration because team members who wouldn't normally cross paths now did.

I also had an employee who hated anything joy or engagement related. He was two years from retirement, which I knew because every morning we would do the same thing. I would say, "Good morning, how are you today?" And he would respond, "Morning, two years and sunny." I thought at first that it was an interesting response to my question, but after a few months, I realized he was talking about his retirement account where he would see sunshine in the top right corner and it would tell him he had two years left to work. Many of our conversations started or ended with him saying something about how he wanted to come and do his work and go home, none of that engagement hooey.

During our monthly potluck, he would complain to other employees, sharing his disdain for the whole thing and finally one day I had had enough. I pulled him aside and said, "You don't like the potluck, I get it." Before I could continue, he said a few more things about why he disliked engagement in general. And then I turned to him and said, "You are two years and sunny. I have people on this team who are 40 years and cloudy...they have a long long time to work ahead of them and they need joy and engagement to get them through. Now I know you don't need any of this hooey, but will you do me a favor and not ruin it for the others?" He grunted a bit and I said thanks and walked away. A few weeks later, I could have fallen over in my chair when I saw him place a casserole dish on the counter for the potluck. He looked at me and said, "What? It's for the kids!" I smiled.

There will be times when engagement or workplace joy feels like it's corny or silly, but that's because it might not be for you. Some people are perfectly content with little or no engagement activities, which is great! For some, it will be a way to pass the time or something to look forward to. I try to remind myself that workplace joy is meant to make the days lighter and brighter. Most of us will work close to 90,000 hours in our careers and that's a lot of hours to not have joy!

Get Curious

I had a colleague once tell me, if you don't like something or someone, that means that you have not spent enough time on it or with them yet. I was struggling to engage one of the people on my team at the time, so I took her advice and took that person to lunch. Over a bowl of noodles, I tried my best to learn about my team members and we both agreed that we were surprised at the things we had in common. I HATE mashed potatoes (it's a texture thing) and so did they. I LOVE traveling, too! Being curious helped me open a window into their world. When I went on my next vacation, I dropped a postcard in the mail to them. A little effort went a long way.

I started to make it my job to be curious about what people do with their spare time, their hobbies, favorite vacation spots, likes and dislikes. Anytime I learned something new, I would jot it down so that from time-to-time I could create a quick moment of joy. I also found that it reminded me to be more joyful.

If someone said they enjoyed collecting stamps, it reminded me of the stamp collection my friend had as a child and I would try to leave a stamp on their desk randomly. If someone mentioned a book or a podcast they were reading, it sparked some inspiration for me to listen to that audiobook and compare thoughts. When one team member said they did nails in their spare time, I asked if I could hire her to do mine for a work event coming up.

Our brains automatically go into work mode, and it can be a welcomed break when you ask about what they enjoy doing outside of work. It also shows that you care more about the person. I encourage you to create more joy at work (big and small).

Joy List Ideas for a Work Setting

- Holiday celebrations (i.e. egg hunt)
- Contests or challenges (i.e mad lib contest)
- Virtual engagement (i.e. bingo via email)
- Sports tailgates or potlucks
- Thought of you (i.e. sending articles to employees – I thought of you)
- Helping others (i.e. sponsoring a non-profit, making sandwiches for a homeless shelter)
- Baby and prom photos

Kid Joy Ideas

When asked what joy ideas they might have for this obstacle, my daughter Alaina (9 years old) and her friend Sawyer (11 years old) came up with these!

I Have Kids

Kids

Being present is the best gift of joy I can give.

Justification – What we tell ourselves.

If you are a parent, you know the little kid stage is hard (sleepless nights, days filled with messy toddlers and moments), and now that we are past those days, I realize the next stage is not any easier (who knew?!). In the recent parenting chapter, we have busy and opinionated elementary and middle school-aged kids, who have ideas about their bedtime, what they wear, and when and what they eat for dinner. Don't even get me started on parenting with technology, that's a whole other book, ha! Our days don't seem to get any easier, and from what I hear from friends with high school-aged children, these challenges are tiny...just wait, they say! I watch as neighbor kids, who were once riding their scooters down the sidewalk, are now hoping into their cars and driving off. My son even said, "mom in three years that will be me."

Obstacles - the permission and perspective we need to overcome.

I look at my parents, family friends, and relatives who are starting to retire saying things like, "Growing old is for the birds" or "I can't quite do the things I used to." I watch as they begin to care for their elderly parents, start making really tough decisions about their health, and the added responsibility and stress that comes with that. I pause on whether any stage has fewer battles and barriers. Either way, I start thinking to myself, when life gives you lemons, you must make lemonade.

Your Turn

For much of COVID, our basement looked like a blanket and pillow bomb had just gone off. We had blankets draped from the table to the couch and back again. At first, we had the rule that the blanket fort had to be picked up, but that was short-lived. A few weeks in, my husband

JOY is My Job

and I gave up. I would find my husband curled up in the fort with the kids watching a movie or playing house. The forts traveled from room to room and got more elaborate each time! Now that COVID has calmed down, my daughter has upped her game and is building box forts in the garage and creating cardboard ice cream stands complete with plastic containers she plans to serve her customers ice cream with this summer. I admire her imagination and sheer ingenuity. If anything, her crazy ideas have reminded me that being present is the best gift of joy I can give.

I, on the other hand, am trying to be more present, specifically with the things my kids like to do. It used to make me crazy to sit down and play pretend, but now I realize that it is a window into their worlds. A sneak peek of who they are becoming. My son loves to play video games and play soccer and my daughter loves to do hair, makeup, and gymnastics. There have been a few mornings where I have answered the doorbell with dark purple eyeshadow which probably made me look like I got punched in the eye. I now play pretend: house and puppies, airplanes where they are the pilot and crew and I am the passenger, and all the silly things that make me cringe a little, but I do it anyway. And little by little each child is realizing that their version of joy is different from that of others and even different than mine. We talk about how, by helping create joy for someone else, we can feel the joy too. It's powerful to be able to give someone the gift of joy.

This principle applies to more than just my kids. My husband loves technology and sports. He has many statistics memorized and loves to dissect new pieces of technology coming out. I used to think it was annoying or boring to listen to these stats, as I am never going to need them, but when I take the time to hear what he has to say, he gets excited and more animated. I can see the joy on his face and the happiness I am helping create for him.

Vacation Planning

One fun family activity we are doing this year for vacation planning is that each person in the family gets to come up with their ideal joyful vacation location. Each of us is developing a PowerPoint of where they would like to go. We have a budget and travel dates to consider. My daughter is currently making her PowerPoint for Mexico and writing a persuasive paper on Las Vegas. My son, who cannot make up his mind either, is making a presentation for both France and Spain. It's been amazing to see a 9-year-old and an 11-year-old think through the options and do their homework and research on the different places. It's been a great way for them to think about finances, whether or not everyone would like an activity, etc.

Joy is messy and imperfect (especially with kids)

The joy you plan to create might turn out to be something completely different, but don't let that get in the way.

One afternoon we took our kids to a movie at a local theater. It was this cute little theater in a nearby neighborhood, where instead of sitting in a traditional movie seat, you sit on barstools with a counter in front of you to watch the movie. The movie times were family-friendly and I envisioned the most perfect movie experience where my kids sat, laughed, and ate popcorn to their heart's content, while my husband and I adoringly looked at how cute they were being. So into the movie we went!

My vision of a stress-free movie ended up looking a little different than expected. Our kids' attention spans waned and they did not last more than 30 minutes before they were jumping off their stools, playing under the counter, tossing popcorn around, and being loud. We exited the theater (my dreams slightly crushed) and when we reached the parking lot, I looked at my husband and said, "This was supposed to be a joy activity, not a hot mess!"

He responded with, "Yeah, I agree. What should we do now? Go home?" We looked at our kids, who were now running around chasing each other in a circle on the grass, and it dawned on me...we had come here to create and joy and, by the looks of two very happy and laughing children, we had succeeded. Our joy mission had been accomplished. Joy can be a little bit messy. The joy you plan to create might turn out to be something completely different, but don't let that get in the way. If you end up pivoting to something completely different than you thought you would be doing, no problem! Life does not go to plan and neither does joy.

Keep it Simple

One thing I found out early in parenting, probably because my husband was in medical school and residency and I was a single mom for a bunch of years, was that sometimes joy comes in the simple moments. Sometimes it's a trip to Target, splashing around in muddy puddles, or picking dandelions. And sometimes it's folding laundry or stacking cups, just so they can knock them over again. As parents, we put a lot of pressure on ourselves to be perfect, get it all done, and feel accomplished, but the dishes in the sink will be there tomorrow and the kids won't notice if the floor is dirty. I try to balance the fact that kids just make life more chaotic and busy, and that does not mean you cannot find time for joy.

Buy Some Painters Tape

I remember buying my first roll of painter's tape and never looking back. Do you know how many things you can do with little kids that are related to painter's tape? We have made obstacle courses, mazes, hopscotch, and treasure hunts where X marked the spot. We have used the tape to hang streamers and paper snowflakes. We mapped out designs on the driveway and colored them in with chalk, we taped each other to the wall for fun and even tossed around the tape ball afterward. If you are looking for an inexpensive way to create joy with kids, painter's tape is a great resource!

Create Monthly Joy

If you are in the "kid season," you will want to get creative about finding joy WITH your kids because as we know, parenting is a 24/7 job. There are times when I just don't have the energy to plan our joy and I have found that leaning on my kids and husband does the trick.

Now that my kids are older, fifth grade and third grade, every month or so we create a list of joy ideas. We make our joy lists on a piece of typing paper and I keep a pile of them hanging on our fridge. My daughter even brought home a list of things to do this summer with her friend, whom she insists on having more playdates with this summer. She even brought me a Post-it note with the girl's mom's cell phone number. I have to smile because it's almost as if she thinks joy is her job!

You would be surprised at the great ideas they have come up with.

Joy List Ideas

- Buy some painter's tape and get creative. Make obstacle courses, mazes, hopscotch, and treasure hunts where X marks the spot
- Paint by sticker
- Arcade
- Learn cursive
- Play chess
- Make donut balls
- Tie-dye shirts
- Play at McDonald's Play Place
- Ask them to brainstorm their ideas!

Kid Joy Ideas

When asked what joy ideas they might have for this obstacle, my daughter Alaina (9 years old) and her friend Sawyer (11 years old) came up with these!

People

Joy is the same; when it comes to joy, tailor it to you.

Justification – What we tell ourselves.

- I'm done people-ing by the time I get home from work
- My spouse is a party pooper
- People drive me bonkers, I don't have the patience
- I am an introvert and want to recharge by myself

Check, check, check. These are all valid reasons why joy might be interrupted by people. However, consider this:

- After work, you can create joy for you
- Create joy without your spouse (not always, but sometimes)
- If you don't have the patience for people, create joy for you or create more joy and see if that makes you a more patient person
- To my introverts who want to recharge by themselves, yes! I highly recommend it

Obstacles - the permission and perspective we need to overcome.

I hate the cold and it never fails that half the soccer season, I am bundled up like a snowman along the side of the field during games. I am contemplating buying one of those weather pop-up spectator pods, which is a plastic tent you sit inside to keep the cold out. Two families had them last year, and though I caught myself judging them at the beginning of the season, by the end I was asking whether they ordered them on Amazon (can't beat em, join em). It makes me feel better thinking that I can control one little piece of the soccer experience, and tailor it to me. Joy is the same; when it comes to joy, tailor it to you.

Your Turn

When I sit down to eat a meal, I love to see a variety of food on my plate and a mix of colors. I cannot imagine what it might be like to eat one thing for every meal, but I am sure it would feel uninspiring. This is the same with creating joy, variety matters.

Joy List Ideas

Normally, I would give you a list of things to do here, but instead, I want you to create a list of the things you like to do for yourself and with others. I have one joy list for myself and my husband has his own, but we also have a list of the things we like to do together. Don't be discouraged if your list is not long, you can build it over time.

- Me
- We

Kid Joy Ideas

When asked what joy ideas they might have for this obstacle, my daughter Alaina (9 years old) and her friend Sawyer (11 years old) came up with these!

PART 3

Joy Framework

Now is the part where I tell you to kick down the barriers to joy and start designing the life of your dreams! We will talk about how to jumpstart your joy, how to normalize joy, what to do when you are not in the mood for joy and finally, we will walk through a framework to create more joy!

Joy will happen without effort, but if you are not intentional with joy, you are leaving potential enjoyment on the table.

Jumpstarting Your Joy

Unfortunately, there is no cookie-cutter way to jumpstart your joy. I tend to do well at something for a while, and then things drop off, like exercise or weight loss. The same holds for joy. You might be great for a little while and then you will realize that joy took a backseat. Instead of feeling like you have failed, say to yourself, "good news, now I am aware and can move joy back up on the priority list." Joy is your job and peaks and valleys are normal, and if you find yourself in a valley, keep moving!

Normalize Joy

I worked in healthcare with neuroscience patients. Colleagues who worked in hospice would always say that the people nearing the end talked about their regrets and how they wished they had spent more time with the people they loved or been more present (life just slipped by). Sure, joy will happen without effort, but if you are not intentional with joy, you are leaving potential enjoyment on the table. It's the memories we take with us (not the money or accolades) — it's those joyful moments.

When I tell people that "Joy is my job," about a third of the people look at me like I am an alien who just flew in from outer space☺. Even though it may SEEM like everyone around you is not prioritizing joy, and they may think you are a bit crazy for doing so, do it anyway. Your life is short and remember, joy is contagious, they may join you after all!

I'm Not in the Mood

There have been times when my husband and I had time plotted out on our joy calendar and then when the day came, we did not feel like it. Like a lot of things in our life, sometimes I'm not in the mood for doing the dishes, cleaning, cooking, or all the house-related items, and frankly, just being an adult.

When those moments hit, acknowledge that feeling and go create joy anyway! Just the other night, I booked a sitter and reservations at a restaurant. We were both sitting at the booth feeling a little slumpy and agreeing that we were not really in the mood for joy, as our week had been busy. The funny thing though, was that just by acknowledging it and sitting with it for a minute, we started to talk about some joy that we had coming up and plans we had on the calendar. Before we knew it, we were laughing and eating and drinking and reminiscing. Sometimes just getting yourself in motion is the key. There is a little bit of gray in between and feeling out of the mood to flip the switch, I call this the muddy middle of joy.

The JOY Framework

*Joy
Framework*

Don't shoot for a specific destination as you create joy, but rather be on a mission to make great memories along the way.

Creating a more joyful life does take a little effort, but only a little, and here is why. As a family, the most difficult part of creating joy at first was thinking of things to do. You would be surprised, but it's easy to be in a rut and stay there. A business coach once gave me the task of writing down 100 things I love and after I had 20 things on my list, I stalled. It became harder to think of things until I got a little more granular and more creative. The same goes for creating a joy list!

Step 1: Give yourself some grace

Give Yourself Some Grace

I have a friend who has a sign business on Etsy and for Christmas one year, I ordered a little wooden sign that now sits next to my husband's nightstand that says, "it's not about the destination, it's about the journey." This is your joy journey. I hope you reach the end of your life and think, what a ride! Don't shoot for a specific destination as you create joy, but rather be on a mission to make great memories along the way. Joy is a feeling that is tied to an action or thought. So as you officially begin chasing joy like it's your j-o-b, remember it is about the journey and not the destination.

In joy sessions all across the country, I have given people topics and challenges to brainstorm joy around and the first thing that happens is they say, "this is harder than I thought!" The reason it feels hard is that it is not "normal" for us yet to chase joy yet, it's not yet a habit. We have not made the tiny shifts in our life for it to feel easy. So give yourself some grace and know that creating your joy list and sticking to a joy calendar will not be easy at first. We have talked about how important mindset can be in creating joy, as well as the barriers that get in our way. Now it's time for you to give yourself some grace and go.

Turn crappy to happy

Crappy to Happy

One of my favorite joy hacks is to look for the crappy and turn it into happiness. What I mean is that there will be things in your life that are unglamorous, annoying, and absolutely no fun. Things you dread doing, but at the end of the day, they have to be done. If I made a list of the crappy things I do in my life, there would be things from work and home written down. Some of my crappy items take a long time to complete and others take no time at all.

Let's talk about housework. One of my crappy to happy activities is matching socks. I don't enjoy it and I think it's a silly activity, but after 10+ years of marriage, I know it's important to my husband and makes him very happy, probably the same way a clean and wiped-down kitchen counter does for me. When I realized that the sock-matching activity was not going away anytime soon, I proudly announced to my husband that I would like to turn this crappy activity into a happy one. Of course, he laughed at me, but I kept it going and now the kids join in too!

Every few days we now host our informal Sock Party! We fold while listening to music, dance around while we fold, or even throw socks over the banister to make it snow. We have ordered pizza a few times and made cookies for the occasion and I always tell my kids, there will be many, many, many unglamorous things you do in your life, but do them with a little fun. These things will seem crappy, like things that you cannot change, but I encourage you to make them a little bit better...put some joy on top of or inside of that activity. If you have to name those activities (like a folding socks party) and listen to music while you do it to make it a little more joyful, so be it.

We don't just stop at socks, we try to get our kids as involved in the chores and household activities as possible. The other day my son made a cooking show on how to make an egg while cooking his breakfast. My daughter made a cooking video about how to make toast. I'm hoping our next video is about how to load the dishwasher, ha!

About a year ago, I was a speaker at a conference, and at the end of the day, there was a social event for speakers and sponsors to gather and grab snacks and a drink. I had an hour's break before I was to speak at a local college in the area, so I made my way over to the event. I did not know anyone, so I made my way over to the bar. There was an extremely well-dressed woman ordering in front of me so I waited. When she turned around, she noticed me and said, "I attended your session today." I looked at her for a minute, bracing myself a bit, and said, "What did you think?"

She turned to me and said, "I visit my mother in the nursing home each week and it's painful. I don't know what to talk with her about and we end up staring at each other and I leave frustrated. Your Crappy to Happy trick was helpful. The next time I visit her, we are going to play Yahtzee, which is a game we used to love playing. Crappy to Happy, right?" And then she walked away. I have never talked to this woman again, but I hope she has turned her crappy into happy...and that maybe she is still pivoting and finding new ways to make visits to her mother more enjoyable.

Step 2: Create a joy list

Have you ever looked at your spouse or friend, on a Friday night, and had a back-and-forth conversation about where to eat? Sometimes it seems to take longer to decide where to go than to actually go. Joy can feel the same without a list. You will NEED a list of joy ideas at the ready, so you don't end up trying to have joy and think of joy ideas at that same moment.

For our family, creating a joy list is as simple as grabbing a sheet of typing paper and writing the word JOY at the top. We usually set a timer for 5-10 minutes and answer this question: What could we do for joy? The first time we made our joy lists, it felt hard, but by our twentieth or thirtieth joy lists, the exercise has gotten much easier. Some of my kids' first joy list ideas included movie nights, game nights, arcade nights, playing soccer, frisbee, and basketball, or making doughnut balls, making tie-dye t-shirts, paint by number, going to the pool, and playing at McDonald's play place. The list of ideas was a great starting point and I loved that the kids were able to put their own stamp on joy. If you have kids, they will too!

After the first 5-10 minutes of brainstorming, I usually give my family another prompter question or two so we can get even more ideas down. Two of my prompter questions are usually to have them add a few free joy list ideas and then I have them brainstorm things we could do for less than $20. Come up with a list of ideas for the home that are free and then things you like to do in the community that are free or low-cost. Activities like trying out a new coffee shop or grabbing a doughnut, something that won't take much effort or income to execute. Joy can happen anytime, and having a grab n' go list will be very helpful! Many of us have busy schedules and need to make it as easy as possible for ourselves so that when the time is right, we can create it without much effort.

In addition to having a paper joy list (don't forget to take a picture of your list on your cell phone, so you always have the list with you), I also have a note in my phone where I can dump joy ideas. Sometimes my kids will come up with a joy idea while we are in the car and when we arrive at our destination, I drop the idea onto that list or they text it to me.

About once a month we come up with fresh joy ideas, find your tempo with creating or adding to your joy list. Having a rhythm helps our brains keep thinking about joy during the in-between times. Even if we have not checked everything off our other joy lists, it helps us keep the momentum.

Step 3: Schedule your joy

Once you have a good batch of joy ideas created, it's time to think about where to put them in your life. I encourage you to grab your calendar, whether it's a piece of paper, a document on your computer, or even a mental piece of paper stored in your mind. Got your calendar in front of you?

Let's take a look. These are just four ways to beef up your calendar with joy.

1. Make the things you already have coming up more joyful or fun.

    a. If you have kids' sports games coming up, plan a tailgate right before it.

b. If you are going to be in the car a lot this month driving kids around to practices or activities, create a goodie bag for yourself so you have joy all ready to go.

c. If there is a holiday already planned, make it even more fun through the food or an activity.

d. If you have a date night scheduled, do something small to make it even more special.

2. Put a new joy idea or two on the calendar, even if you have to schedule it out a bit.

    a. If you look at your joy list and realize you don't have any time to squeeze things in, go to a spot on the calendar where things clear out a bit and put a couple of holds on the calendar for joy.

    b. Schedule in batches of three. I notice that if I schedule one joy item on my calendar, I am not good at coming back and scheduling another one and a bunch of time goes by. So I have trained myself to schedule joy in batches of three. I put three joy items on the calendar (sometimes with a fun theme) so it feels like less work to plan.

3. Look at the befores and afters.

    I love to scan my calendar and look for 30- to 60-minute spots of the before or after of things to put in joy. If I am going to have a busy day with lots of things going on, I try to use the time before for a little joy, even if it is a cup of coffee on my porch for 10 minutes. Use those little bits of time for joy. Put holds on your calendar so you have the space to enjoy!

4. Crappy to Happy

As I mentioned earlier, taking the things that are unglamorous, annoying, and absolutely no fun, or the things you dread doing but need to get done at the end of the day, and making them happier is your job. You have to take crappy and make it happy.

For example, that spreadsheet might take you half the afternoon, so reward yourself during or when it's finished. After cleaning the bathroom, I might take 10 or 15 minutes of "me time" to read a book, do a crossword, or watch trashy TV and not feel any guilt whatsoever. My husband and I have opposite golden hours of the day, he is a night owl and I am a morning person, so our crappy to happy times don't align. He would rather do the dishes at 11 pm and I would rather wake up in the morning, clean the kitchen and start my day.

Think about those crappy things in your day and identify them on your calendar. Now put something with it or alongside it that will bring you joy. Take your crappy to happy!

That is what joy is all about, just dreaming and doing. Some of your ideas will work out and others won't, but it's the journey that matters, not the destination.

Step 4: Let's GO!   Let's Go!

When I was little, I was convinced of many things, some possible and some impossible. For example, I believed that:

1. I could dig a hole to China
2. I would move to New York City one day
3. I would have five dogs when I grew up
4. I would be a famous singer and own horses

5. The man on the moon was real and if I stared hard enough, I could catch a glimpse of him

The thing about being a little kid is that you believe without any proof or possibility. You don't need evidence or approval, you just know. We are born believing that we CAN; that if we head in the general direction, someday we will get there. We don't do a cost-benefit analysis or even think about what would be needed to make it happen, and then just maybe...finally decide if the juice is worth the squeeze. Instead, we let our minds dream and just figure it out as we go along. That is what joy is all about, just dreaming and doing. Some of your ideas will work out and others won't, but it's the journey that matters, not the destination.

Conclusion

Quick status update, I am 37 years old and:

1. I never dug a hole to China.
2. I never moved to New York City but did spend time living in Chicago and Milwaukee.
3. I had one dog, an adorably friendly and barky black dachshund. And as life would have it, one of our kids ended up being allergic to her and so our pet career has come to an end.
4. My singing career never got off the ground and neither did my horse-owning adventure. Although I still have horseback riding on my joy list for next year.
5. I have yet to spot the man on the moon, but I am still hopeful that SOMEDAY, I will catch a glimpse. You gotta believe, right?

I invite you to stay hopeful and intentional about creating joy in the day-to-day moments of your life and keep dreaming. Put some things on paper and just go!

As the final takeaway from this book, I challenge you to start heading in the general direction of joy...just chase it...you never know how things will end up and life might turn out sweeter and more joyful than you could ever imagine! If you wait around for joy to find you, it might never happen.

What are you waiting for? I am cheering for you! Now, get out there and create more joy LIKE IT'S YOUR JOB!

If you have an amazing joy idea to share, go to lisaeven.com to share it with me!

Link to freebies/further resources: https://www.lisaeven.com/freejoy

A Quick Joy Check-in

Joy Check In

You made it! Let's see where you are now!

Creating more joy tomorrow starts with a check-in on where you are today. Take a bit of time to reflect on the current status of your joy, and then answer the three questions below. The answers to these questions will be the catalyst for building a life filled with joy!

(1) What are currently the top three things that get in your way of having joy?

4. _____

5. _____

6. _____

(2) If you were to look ahead one year from now, what area(s) of your life would you want to see more joy in?

_____

_____

_____

On a scale of 1-10, where are you <u>currently</u> on the joy scale?

LOW ☹   HIGH ☺

1   2   3   4   5   6   7   8   9   10

"If you always do what you've always done,
you'll always be where you've always been." ~ T.D.

Discussion Questions

1. What are the top three things that get in your way of having joy? And why?

2. If you were to look ahead one year from now, what area(s) of your life would you want to see more joy in? And why?

3. What do you believe about joy? Use some of these prompters (and your own) to help you sort through your current joy perspective.

    a. Are joy and happiness the same?
    b. When I experience something sad, can I also have joy?
    c. I have to finish (insert goal or milestone) and then things will be better, and more joyful.
    d. Money prevents me from having joy.
    e. I let my lack of creativity (not a Pinterest person) get in the way of joy.
    f. Is joy a habit you create?

4. What does permitting yourself to have more joy look like for you?

5. In what areas of your life can you turn crappy into happy? Not sure what this means, go back and read that section in the book.

6. What do you need to do to create a joy mindset?

7. What ideas can you add to your joy list?

8. Do you believe that joy is Your Job?

About the Author

Eight years ago, I was chasing... to keep up with my career, my kids, the housework, my email, you name it. And then it hit me, I (along with my family) had been making everything else our job, except for joy.

I turned to my husband with a crazy idea and said, "What if we make joy our jobs? I have a feeling that if we wait for joy to find us, we might wait forever. Let's look at our life and start infusing joyful activities inside our busy and hectic days."

Armed with an idea and half a plan, we put joy at the top of our list. We started creating a joy-filled mindset, moments, and experiences. I am excited to share all of that with you in this book.

By day, I am a keynote speaker, success coach, and joy connoisseur, who has helped countless people transform their personal and professional lives to create more JOY and Have Good Ripple Effect via keynote speaking, coaching, workshops, newsletters, and public appearances.

By night, I am a mom, wife, daughter, sister, neighbor, and friend, who is on a mission to create more joy and laughter along the way.

You can find more out about me and sign up for my newsletter at lisaeven.com.

Made in United States
Troutdale, OR
12/30/2024

27380827R00076